Alan Feduccia

THE AGE OF
BIRDS

Harvard University Press

Cambridge, Massachusetts, and London, England • 1980

Library of Congress Cataloging in Publication Data

Feduccia, J Alan.
  The age of birds.

  Bibliography: p.
  Includes index.
  1. Birds—Evolution. 2. Birds—Classification.
3. Birds, Fossil. I. Title.
QL677.3.F42   598   80-11926
ISBN 0-674-00975-4

To Olivia

Contents

Preface

In this book I have tried to tell the story of the evolution of birds in a way that will appeal to people of diverse interests. Rather than analyzing every avian fossil and living species of bird, I have included only enough detail to explore important issues in avian evolution and phylogeny. Some of the ideas expressed in this book are new ones that have not yet withstood the test of time, but my aim has been to provide the reader with more than the static dogma of the past century. And while I must acknowledge a large debt to a number of colleagues, many of the points of view put forth in the following pages are mine alone.

Much of this book was written while I was on a Kenan Leave from the University of North Carolina at the Smithsonian's National Museum of Natural History. I am extremely grateful to the staff of the Division of Birds of the Smithsonian Institution for their help, especially Storrs L. Olson, who provided not only office and laboratory facilities, but also stimulating and challenging conversation and debate.

Among the many people who have given me information and helpful criticism, I should like to thank especially: Robert J. Raikow, who allowed me to examine parts of his unpublished manuscript on the pelvis of ratites; Kenneth E. Campbell, Jr., who let me read his manuscript on the largest teratorn; and Walter H. Wheeler, who advised me on the usage of geological terms. I am particularly grateful to Charles R. Blake, Pierce Brodkorb, John Farrand, Jr., and Larry D. Martin for reading and commenting on the entire manuscript. Stevie Glass Champion helped in editing and typing parts of an early draft. William Patrick and Nancy N. Clemente of Harvard University Press edited the manuscript with great skill and expertly led it through the various stages of production.

The artists and photographers who provided illustrations are acknowledged in the figure captions. But I would like to thank especially John P. O'Neill, who executed the first life reconstruction of *Presbyornis* for Chapter 5. I am also very grateful to the staff of the National Museum of Natural History's scanning electron microscope facility, Walter R. Brown, Mary-Jacque Man, and Susann G. Braden, who helped prepare the scanning electron micrographs used in this book.

Chapel Hill, North Carolina
April 1980

We are not here concerned with hopes or fears, only with the truth as far as our reason permits us to discover it.

—CHARLES DARWIN

Reconstruction of *Archaeopteryx*.
(Painting by Rudolf Freund; courtesy
of the Carnegie Museum of Natural
History.)

The Feathered Reptile

1

At a time when tropical temperatures warmed much of the Northern Hemisphere, and low, palmlike vegetation covered what is now central Europe, a feathered creature the size of a crow met its death in a shallow lagoon. Of the event itself this is all we can know, separated from us as it is by approximately 140 million years. But the death was recorded nonetheless, chronicled by sediments that, through the millennia, settled and consolidated into lithographic limestone, a fine-grained stone that retained not only the shape of bones, but the delicate impression of feathers. The creature thus memorialized was *Archaeopteryx lithographica,* and while indisputably birdlike, it could with equal truth be called reptilian. The forearms that once held feathers outstretched had solid, reptilian bones and ended in claws of three fingers. The *Archaeopteryx* fossil is, in fact, the most superb example of a specimen perfectly intermediate between two higher groups of living organisms—what has come to be called a "missing link." Its discovery in 1861, just two years after publication of Charles Darwin's *On the Origin of Species,* seemed an unparalleled act of cosmic good will toward science. For by fulfilling the Darwinian expectation that such intermediate forms exist, this one fossil had a profound influence on the acceptance of the concept of evolution through natural selection. And for students of avian evolution, *Archaeopteryx* became the focal point of efforts to determine the descent of birds.

In attempting to construct a genealogical history, or phylogeny, for birds, we must look both to living forms and to the fossil record of ancient birds. *Archaeopteryx,* the oldest avian form yet discovered, is represented by five specimens, one of which is almost perfectly preserved. But the fossil record is rarely so cooperative. Most bird bones are hollow—an adaptation that lightened the skeleton for flight—and are therefore not easily preserved. An extreme example of this is seen in the frigatebird, whose feathers, it is said, probably weigh more than the dried skeleton. Most bird fossils are also fragmentary, or consist of single bones, and it is only the rare find of an associated skeleton that allows major advances in the effort to establish evolutionary relationships.

Another difficulty in discussing avian phylogeny is that, beneath their feathers, birds tend to be very much alike. For example, in order for flight to be possible, the forelimbs had to assume an elongated form in the first birds, and they have retained that form with very little modification in all modern birds. By contrast, mammals possess many features, such as teeth, that differ substantially among the various groups and indicate evolutionary relationships. Traits of the major avian groups present very few such clues.

Because of the extreme physiological demands of flight, birds are finely tuned metabolic machines, with high metabolic rates (the highest of all vertebrates). Many anatomical features are also unique to modern birds and have evolved as adaptations for flight. The pneumatic bones already mentioned are complemented by an extensive air-sac system throughout the avian body that extends into certain of the hollow bones, such as the humerus. Modern birds also exhibit a great deal of deletion and fusion of bones, more so than any other group of living vertebrates, adaptations again associated with lightening of the skeleton for flight.

One of the first features the birds' reptilian predecessors lost was teeth; and apparently the bone that was armed with them, the maxilla, also disappeared. These were replaced by the lighter bill. Even the sex organs were reduced to decrease weight: most females have only one ovary, and many males lack a penis, although a modified penis has been reacquired by some large flightless birds.

The avian body is very compact. Virtually all the major skull bones are fused into a single rigid structure, the wing and leg bones are reduced in number, and many elements are fused. In the wing, for example, there are three instead of the normal five fingers of the vertebrate hand, and the three carpal bones are fused to form the avian carpometacarpus. From this three-fingered hand emerge the primary flight feathers, numbering from 9 to 12 in flying birds; from the ulnar region come the secondary flight feathers. Collectively, these feathers are called the remiges. In the leg the three tarsal bones are fused to form the avian tarsometatarsus, so that birds actually walk on their toes, and not on their "feet," as we do. Other fusion has taken place in the vertebral column, the sacral vertebrae, for example, having joined to form a solid synsacrum. To add further rigidity to the skeleton, the ribs are equipped with uncinate processes, small bony struts that bind the rib cage together. The clavicles are fused to form the structure called the furcula, or wishbone; this uniquely avian trait stabilizes the shoulder joint and prevents collapse of the frontal region in flight. In all birds but the first, *Archaeopteryx,* the tail vertebrae are reduced and fused into a small blunt pygostyle, from which the tail feathers (rectrices) emanate.

The sternum is highly modified to accommodate the flight muscles. Along its midline is a large bony expanse called the keel, or carina

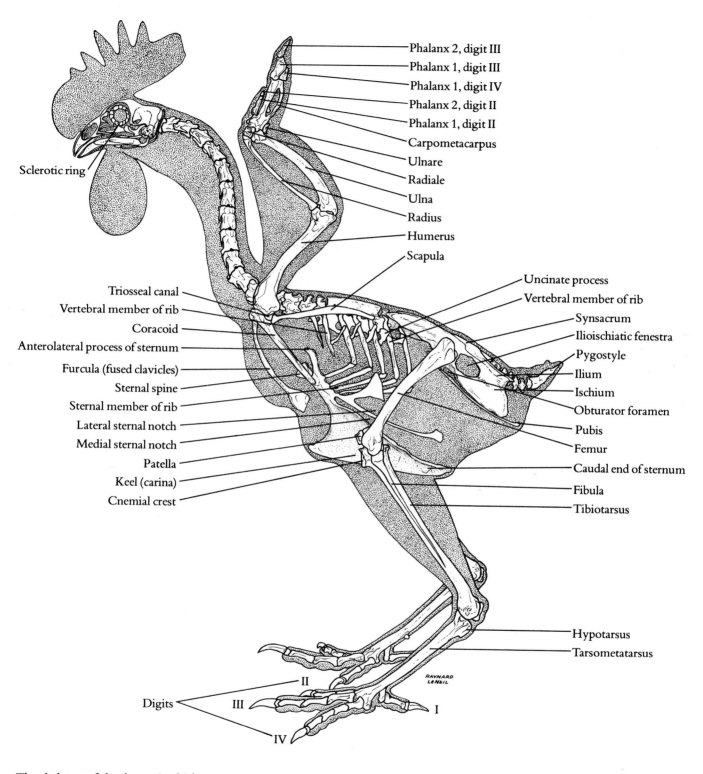

The skeleton of the domestic chicken, showing the major features of avian anatomy. (Adapted from Lucas and Stettenheim, 1972; courtesy of Alfred M. Lucas.)

Comparison of the skeletons of *Archaeopteryx* (*A*) and a modern pigeon (*B*). Comparable regions of the skeleton (braincase, hand, sternum, rib, pelvis, tail) are shaded black. In modern birds, the tail is reduced and several terminal vertebrae fuse to form the pygostyle; the braincase is expanded and the head bones are fused; the hand bones are fused to form a carpometacarpus and the fingers are reduced; the pelvic girdle is joined to the fused sacral vertebrae (the synsacrum); the ribs are bound rigidly by uncinate processes; and the sternum is greatly expanded and is keeled for the attachment of the major flight muscles. All are adaptations associated with perfecting the flight mechanism. (Reprinted, by permission, from E. H. Colbert, *Evolution of the Vertebrates,* copyright 1969 by John Wiley & Sons.)

(Latin, keel of a ship), that provides a broad base for the attachment of the flight muscles. The muscle most responsible for raising the wing for the recovery stroke in modern birds is the large supracoracoideus, and it has unusual features that allow it to perform this function. Originating in the lower region of the carina, it extends up the sternum and is connected to the humerus by a tendon that passes through the triosseal canal formed by the conjunction of the coracoid, the scapula, and the furcula. Thus the supracoracoideus muscle is firmly anchored to both the carina and the humerus, and by running a tendon over a pulley in the shoulder, it does most of the work needed to raise the wing in flight. If it did not, the dorsal elevators, small muscles on the back of the body associated with the scapula, would have to perform this task by themselves. Indeed, in early birds, such as *Archaeopteryx,* that had not yet evolved the supracoracoideus, the dorsal muscles of the scapula were solely responsible for effecting the recovery stroke. In birds that literally fly through the water, and are among the "best" fliers, such as penguins and auks, these dorsal muscles increase in mass, with a concomitant increase in the size of the blade of the scapula.

The massive pectoralis muscle pulls the wing down for the power stroke in flight. It arises partly from the sternum, but mostly from the front and sides of the furcula and adjacent membranes. Together, the powerful pectoralis and supracoracoideus muscles may account for as much as 16 percent of the weight of a mourning dove and 30 percent of the weight of certain hummingbirds.

Despite the unique avian morphology that makes the evolution of birds so difficult to trace, birds themselves have made an enormous contribution to evolutionary theory. The countless varieties of domestic pigeons first led Darwin to contemplate the potential for variability within natural populations. The Galápagos finches, now known as Darwin's finches, offered the first vivid illustration of the transformation of populations. The diurnal habits and easy observability of birds have made them the principal subjects of the research on which most of our knowledge of animal behavior is based. Nonetheless, the specific ancestry of birds and the evolutionary relationships of their major groups are two of the least well-known areas in our understanding of the vertebrates.

How do we proceed, then, in making evolutionary comparisons? We know that during various geological periods birds have appropriated new habitats and biological roles—a phenomenon known as adaptive radiation—and this has resulted in birds' having become modified for particular life-styles, such as diving, wading, and perching. When similar modifications occur in different lineages, the various birds, though unrelated, may come to resemble each other structurally through convergent evolution. We can speak of convergent evolution as applying to the whole organism or to specific features. Examples of whole-organism convergence in birds are legion, and include the ancient, toothed, diving hesperornithids and the modern loons, two groups that evolved foot-propelled diving completely independently of each other, as well as several independently evolved lines of wing-propelled divers, such as penguins, diving petrels, and auks. In many other cases, we can trace the convergence of specific parts of organisms. The typical avian foot, as exemplified by a chicken, has three toes in front and one behind, a condition known as anisodactyly. But in a number of unrelated groups there has evolved a yoke-toed foot termed zygodactyl, with two toes in front and two behind, the outer front toe having reversed itself. Unrelated birds with zygodactyl feet include woodpeckers, cuckoos, and parrots.

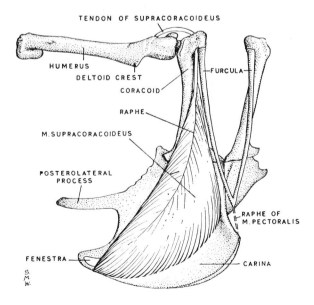

A front (anterior and lateral) view of the sternum and pectoral girdle of the domestic pigeon, showing the general relationship of the supracoracoideus muscle and its tendon of insertion. The tendon passes through the triosseal (three-bone) canal formed by the articulation of the furcula, coracoid, and scapula (not shown here). The supracoracoideus is the major muscle used to raise the wing in flight in modern birds. The pectoralis muscle, which powers the wing in flight, has been removed; it arises partly from the area of the sternum not occupied by the supracoracoideus, but mostly from the front and side surfaces of the furcula and adjacent membranes. (From George and Berger, 1966.)

PELICAN

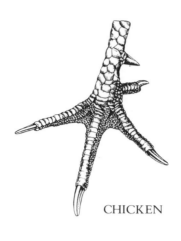

CHICKEN

WOODPECKER

STILT

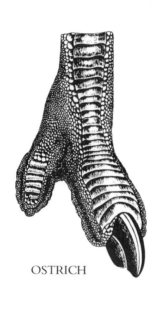

OSTRICH

GROUSE

Examples of the diversity in shape and structure of bird feet and bills produced by adaptive radiation. (From Lucas and Stettenheim, 1972; courtesy of Alfred M. Lucas.)

KINGFISHER

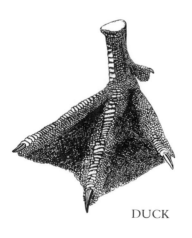

DUCK

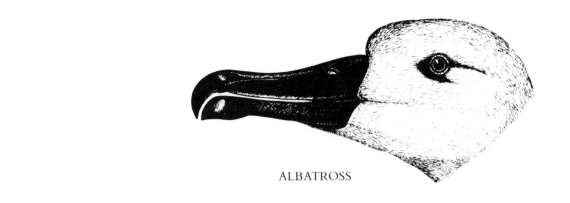

ALBATROSS

SWAN

PUFFIN

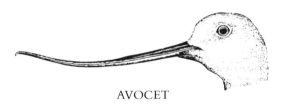

AVOCET

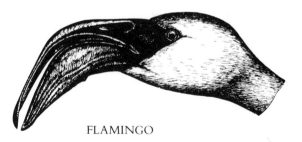

FLAMINGO

GIANT PETREL

SHRIKE

Examples of convergent evolution: above are two unrelated look-alikes among the foot-propelled divers, the ancient, toothed bird *Hesperornis* (*A*) and the modern loon (*B*); below are two look-alikes among the wing-propelled divers, a diving petrel (*C*) and an auk (*D*). (Adapted from Fisher and Peterson, 1964.)

A

B

C

D

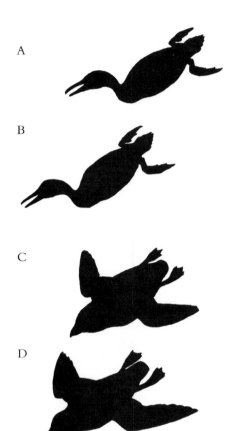

When comparing the structural features, or morphology, of birds in order to reconstruct phylogenies, we must ascertain whether similar structures are homologous, meaning that they can be traced back to a similar condition in a hypothetical common ancestor; or convergent, and therefore not indicative of evolutionary relationships. Other comparisons may involve function rather than structure. The wings of insects and the wings of birds, for example, are two quite different structural approaches to the same function, namely flight. Such functionally related but structurally different features are called analogues.

In comparing structural features it is most useful to be able to determine which characteristics are primitive, that is, are actually present in the hypothetical common ancestor; and which are "derived," that is, have evolved in lineages after branching from the common ancestor. Both robins and cuckoos have similar feathers, for example, but this characteristic does not indicate that the two groups shared an immediate common ancestor—the same feathers were also present in the very first bird. On the other hand, robins and finches share a peculiar sperm structure not found outside their order; it no doubt evolved after the order branched from an ancestor and does represent a derived characteristic that links robins and finches.

In making evolutionary comparisons within birds, historically important characteristics have been skeletal features, such as the sternum and the conformation of the bones of the palate, the pelvic and jaw musculature, the arrangement of the carotid arteries, the pattern of the convolutions of the intestinal tract, the arrangement of the foot tendons and wing feathers, the condition of the external openings of the nasal cavities, certain features of the tarsus and foot, the arrangement of the toes, the muscles of the voice box (syrinx), the pattern of the feather tracts, and the color of the downy young. Recently, behavioral as well as physiological and biochemical comparisons of living birds have been made.

But the phylogeny of a group of organisms is constructed by the study of fossil as well as living forms. It is the fossil record that allows us to place organisms and their lineages on the geological time scale (shown on page 9), and permits us to see changes in diversity and morphology through time. *Archaeopteryx,* for example, lived in the late Jurassic Period, and was preserved in what geologists call upper Jurassic limestone—the terms, "early," "middle," and "late" indicate time, while "lower," "middle," and "upper" refer to the actual rock strata. The comparison shown earlier of *Archaeopteryx,* 140 million years old, with the modern pigeon shows dramatic differences in their shape and structure. In addition, paleontological data also provide evidence on rates of evolution, extinction, and times of major adaptive innovations. But as we have seen, the fossil heritage of birds is incomplete and difficult to interpret. Nonetheless, we do have an excellent starting point, *Archaeopteryx,* and this good fortune appears all the

Geological time scale in millions of years before the present.

Era	Period	Epoch	Million years before present
CENOZOIC (AGE OF BIRDS AND MAMMALS)	QUATERNARY	Recent	0.01
		Pleistocene	
			1.5–3.5
	TERTIARY	Pliocene	
			7
		Miocene	
			26
		Oligocene	
			37–38
		Eocene	
			53–54
		Paleocene	
			65
MESOZOIC (AGE OF REPTILES)	CRETACEOUS	Late	
			100
		Early	
			135
	JURASSIC	Late	
			155
		Middle	
			170
		Early	
			180–190
	TRIASSIC		230

more exceptional when we consider the circumstances of the specimens' fossilization and discovery.

Each of the five specimens of *Archaeopteryx* was recovered from the Solnhofen limestone of the Altmühl region of Bavaria. A great variety of plants, invertebrates, fishes, and reptiles shared this resting place, and they allow us to form some idea of the late Jurassic habitat and the conditions that led to this wealth of fossils. If we picture the shallow lagoons fringed with flats of viscous, calcareous muds, exceptionally low tides and strong offshore winds, it is easy to imagine marine organisms becoming stranded in the mire. Storms would have blown parts of trees, flying insects, the flying reptiles called pterosaurs or pterodactyls, as well as an occasional *Archaeopteryx,* into the lagoons (De Beer, 1954). The fine sediments sealed the fate of these organisms and, with each passing age, formed a new layer of lithographic stone.

Solnhofen limestone has been quarried since Roman times to pave highways and to build homes. Even today all but the most modern buildings in the Altmühl region are finished with floors and roofs of this fine stone. In the nineteenth century, the stone began to be quarried for another purpose, use in the lithographic printing process. New sites were opened, and more important, workers began to check each slab meticulously for its intrinsic quality. It was only such a careful mining process that made the discovery of *Archaeopteryx* possible.

In 1861 Hermann von Meyer of Frankfurt wrote to H. G. Brown, German publisher of the *New Yearbook of Mineralogy,* that a fossil bird

Reconstruction of the late Jurassic shoreline of European lagoons that produced the Solnhofen limestone of Bavaria. Here *Archaeopteryx* is shown with the chicken-sized coelurosaurian dinosaur *Compsognathus* and the tailed Jurassic pterosaur *Rhamphorhynchus*. The Solnhofen deposits preserved 29 species of pterosaurs, ranging from the size of a sparrow to 4 feet in length (*Rhamphorhynchus*), a variety of insects from moths to flies, crustaceans, ammonites, and soft-bodied jellyfish, very rarely preserved as fossils. (Mural by Charles R. Knight; courtesy of the Field Museum of Natural History, Chicago.)

One of the Solnhofen limestone quarries still active today. (Courtesy of John H. Ostrom and the Peabody Museum of Natural History, Yale University.)

had been discovered in a quarry near the village of Solnhofen, not far from Munich. The first specimen, though, was merely a single feather. Blackish in color, 60 millimeters long and 11 millimeters wide, the feather had a vane on one side of the quill that was roughly half as wide as that on the other—the same contours as the flight feathers of modern birds. The implications of this avian hint from the late Jurassic began to resonate. And within a month Meyer was reporting the discovery of a complete fossil skeleton in another quarry not far from the original site. It had a long reptilian tail exhibiting many vertebrae, but attached to each there was what appeared to be a pair of short feathers. The stone had captured these subtle impressions, as well as the startling image of feathered wings. Here clearly was a mosaic of avian and reptilian characteristics. Had it not been for the serendipitous role of the uniquely fine-grained stone, the creature would have been classified as a reptile. Instead, Meyer gave it the avian genus name "ancient wing" (*archaios,* ancient; *pteryx,* wing) and the species designation *lithographica.*

The main slab of the single feather impression went to the Museum of the Academy of Sciences in Munich; the counterslab made its way to the Humboldt Museum für Naturkunde, now in East Berlin. But in 1861, with Victorian science on the march and *On the Origin of*

The first piece of evidence that birds existed in late Jurassic times was the single feather reported by Hermann von Meyer in 1861. Note that the two sides (vanes) of the feather are asymmetric, an arrangement found elsewhere only in the primary flight feathers and outer tail feathers of modern flying birds. Thus evidence of *Archaeopteryx'* ability to fly has been available for more than a hundred years. The main slab is shown above, the counterslab below. (Main slab courtesy of John H. Ostrom; counterslab courtesy of Hermann Jaeger and the Humboldt Museum für Naturkunde, East Berlin.)

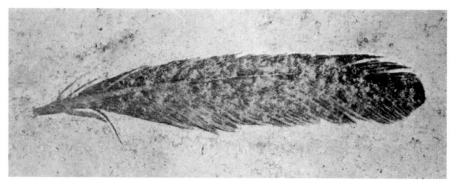

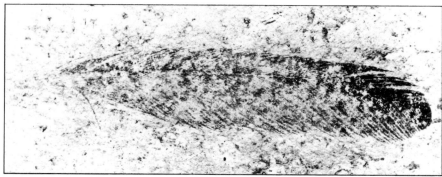

Species two years in print, the complete skeleton, a specimen purported to be an intermediate form between two higher groups of animals, was not to be quietly reinterred in packing cases and catalogued into obscurity.

Many laymen of the time were amassing extensive collections of fossils from the Solnhofen quarries. Likewise, the quarry hands were making profits selling their finds. Dr. Karl Häberlein, a medical officer for the district of Pappenheim, was a collector who accepted fossils in payment for his medical services. In this way, *Archaeopteryx* soon passed into his hands. A speculator at heart, Dr. Häberlein offered the fossil for sale after only three months. All across Europe a mad scramble began, involving royal councilors and learned professors. The German court tried to obtain the curious specimen for the State Collection in Munich. This effort met with the objections of an influential professor of zoology at Munich University named J. Andreas Wagner. Wagner was a staunch opponent of the new Darwinian theory, and he vehemently opposed the idea that there might be a transitional link between reptiles and birds. He expressed his sentiments in a paper pre-

The first complete fossil skeleton of *Archaeopteryx,* known as the London specimen. It was discovered in 1861, shortly after the isolated feather, and it proved the existence of a reptile-bird. It also provided the eminent Darwinian Thomas Huxley with an intermediate form linking reptiles and birds. The London specimen shows clearly the furcula, indicated by the arrow, characteristic of modern flying birds. (Courtesy of the Trustees of the British Museum, Natural History.)

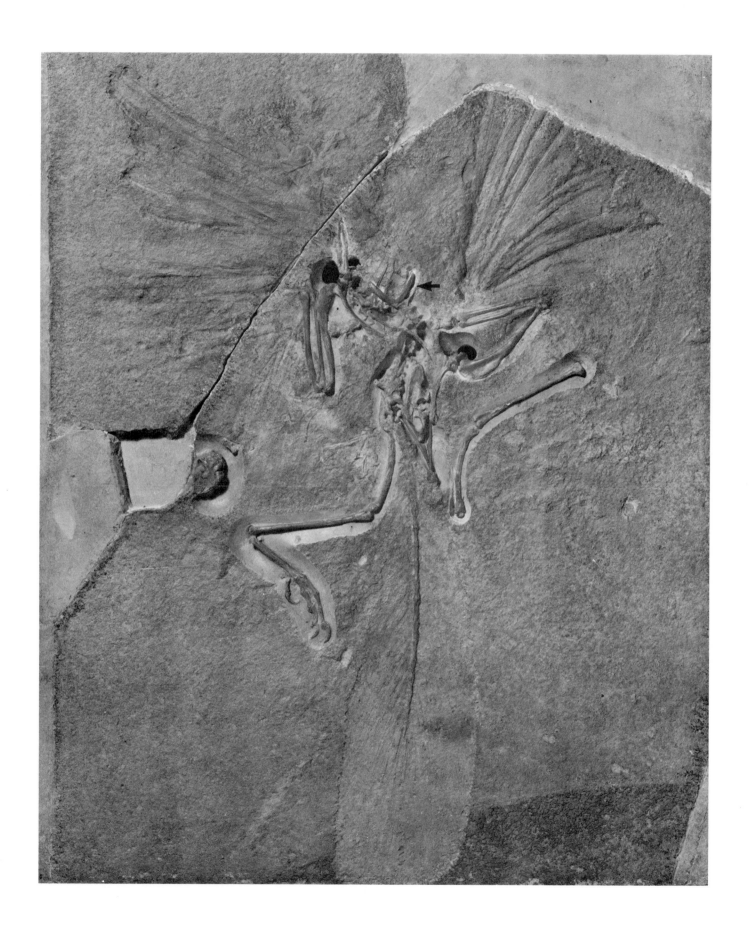

sented to the Munich Academy of Science in 1861 and aptly titled "A New Reptile Supposedly Furnished with Bird Feathers" ("Uber Ein neues, augeblich mit Vogelfedern versehenes Reptil"). Wagner also ignored Meyer's avian name for the fossil and gave it the reptilian designation *Griphosaurus* (*gryps,* mythical beast; *sauros,* lizard).

Meanwhile, Dr. Häberlein was protecting his investment by preserving the aura of mystery that shrouded *Archaeopteryx.* He allowed no one to make any drawings of the fossil, but he did let a few people inspect it in order to dispel rumors that it might be a fake. One of the inspectors later sketched from memory a very accurate rendition. This was shown to Wagner, but he remained adamant in his position that birds did not exist as far back as the late Jurassic.

The significance of *Archaeopteryx* was not wasted on the British. Despite his confirmed antievolutionist position, Sir Richard Owen, Superintendent of the British Museum (Natural History), along with George Robert Waterhouse, Keeper of the Geology Department, recommended that the trustees of the British Museum bid for the prize. After haggling for several months, Häberlein agreed to sell *Archaeopteryx* as well as 1,703 other specimens from his collection for the sum of £700, and the controversial fossil arrived in London in November 1862.

The image of *Archaeopteryx* as a link between reptiles and birds was not readily embraced either by the public or by the scientific community. The obvious implications for a theory of evolution were far too disturbing, especially to the entrenched ecclesiastical view that reptiles and birds were static groups placed on earth in their present unchanging forms.

The debate in England squared off between two main protagonists: Owen, the acknowledged leader of British science and an intimate of the royal family, and Thomas Henry Huxley, the most eloquent defender of Darwin and evolutionary theory. Owen carefully studied the fossil and in 1864 insisted on giving it yet another name, *Archaeopteryx macrura* (long-tailed). While he was at work, three brief papers supporting his views were being published in England, one by Henry Woodward in the *Intellectual Observor,* one translation of a paper by Hermann von Meyer, and a translation of Wagner's paper of 1861. Never having seen the actual fossil, Wagner remained confident in his classification of it as a pterodactyl, a long-tailed flying reptile:

> In conclusion, I must add a few words to ward off Darwinian misinterpretation of our new saurian. At the first glance of the Griphosaurus [*Archaeopteryx*] we might certainly form a notion that we have before us an intermediate creature, engaged in the transition from the saurian to the bird. Darwin and his adherents will probably employ the new discovery as an exceedingly welcome occurrence for the justification of their strange views upon the transformation of animals but in this they will be wrong. (Wagner, 1862, p. 266)

Huxley was also studying the specimen, but in comparison with the smallest known dinosaur, the chicken-sized *Compsognathus* (*kompsos,* elegant; *gnathos,* jaw), which also had been described from the Solnhofen limestone by Wagner (1861b). Huxley found elegant proof of intermediate forms in the birdlike reptile *Compsognathus* and the reptilelike bird *Archaeopteryx,* and his argument was compelling. Even in America professors of natural history were coming around to the Darwinian view, bolstered by this new evidence. As Professor Othniel Charles Marsh of Yale University wrote in 1877:

> The classes of Birds and Reptiles, as now living, are separated by a gulf so profound that a few years since it was cited by the opponents of evolution as the most important break in the animal series, and one which that doctrine could not bridge over. Since then, as Huxley has clearly shown, this gap has been virtually filled by the discovery of bird like Reptiles and reptilian Birds. *Compsognathus* and *Archaeopteryx* of the Old World . . . are the stepping stones by which the evolutionist of to-day leads the doubting brother across the shallow remnant of the gulf, once thought impassable. (p. 352)

But even Thomas Huxley, who later proposed a complete classification of all living birds based on the structure of the bony palate, could not accept the presence in the jaws of *Archaeopteryx* of teeth, a reptilian carry-over. The London specimen was somewhat disarticulated, and as late as 1868 Huxley wrote that the skull was lost. But in fact there remained part of the upper jaw with four teeth, as Sir John Evans had pointed out in 1865 in an article on the cranium and jaw preserved in the fossil slab. Evans fully accepted *Archaeopteryx* as a link between reptiles and birds, but in the same article quoted a letter Hermann von Meyer had written him expressing the anti-Darwinian view that still prevailed in many circles:

> It would appear that the jaw really belongs to the *Archaeopteryx* and arming the jaw with teeth would contradict the view of the *Archaeopteryx* being a bird or an embryonic form of bird. But after all, I do not believe that God formed His creatures after the systems devised by our philosophical wisdom. Of the classes of birds and reptiles as we define them, the Creator knows nothing, and just as little of a prototype, or of a constant embryonic condition of the bird, which might be recognized in the *Archaeopteryx.* The *Archaeopteryx* is of its kind just as perfect a creature as other creatures, and if we are not able to include this fossil animal in our system, our shortsightedness is alone to blame. (1865, p. 421)

The controversy over *Archaeopteryx* continued.

In 1877, while scientists all over the world were still debating the significance of the London *Archaeopteryx,* news of the discovery of another skeletal specimen was announced. This second fossil came from a Solnhofen quarry on the Blumenberg River, near Eichstätt, about 10 miles from the site of the original discoveries, and again it fell into the

Reconstruction of *Compsognathus,* the smallest dinosaur, shown holding a tiny pterodactyl. The dinosaur's head was no more than 3 inches long, and its tail was longer than the entire body. Its tiny jaws were armed with rows of sharp teeth used to devour the small lizards and insects it caught. *Compsog-* *nathus* coexisted with the large dinosaurian flesh-eaters; with members of its own family, the coelurosaurs, many about 6 feet or so long; and with several kinds of ancient mammals. (From *Album of Dinosaurs* by Tom McGowen, illustrated by Rod Ruth; copyright 1972 by Rand McNally & Co.)

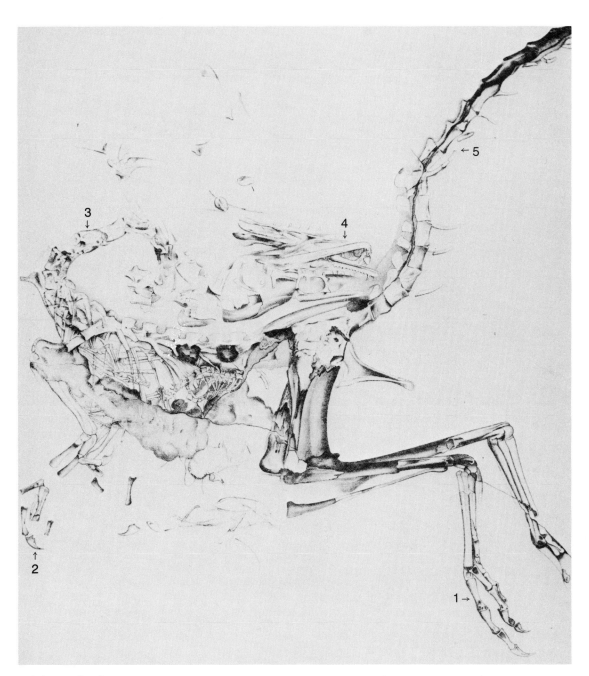

A lithograph of *Compsognathus,* preserved in much the same position as the Berlin specimen of *Archaeopteryx.* The arrows show: *1,* feet; *2,* hand with claws; *3,* neck vertebrae; *4,* head, inverted (arrow points to lower jaw, upside down); *5,* vertebrae of tail. Note the bones of a small lizard preserved in the stomach region. This drawing was made on a slab of Solnhofen limestone from the same general vicinity and deposits from which *Compsognathus* was recovered. The drawing was made some time between 1882 and 1899, and the stone was stored in the vertebrate paleontology collections of Yale's Peabody Museum of Natural History, where it lay unheeded until 1961, when John H. Ostrom rediscovered it. The lithograph was hand-printed in 1977 by Heddi Seibel of the Yale University School of Art. (Courtesy of John H. Ostrom and the Peabody Museum of Natural History, Yale University.)

hands of a speculator—none other than the son of the original *Archaeopteryx* huckster, Dr. Karl Häberlein. Häberlein *fils* immediately advertised the fossil for sale, and this time, the Germans, embarrassed at having lost the first skeleton to the British Museum, were determined to come up with the necessary funds.

Four years of negotiations followed, involving private endowments, the Prussian Ministry of Culture, and numerous men of science. Ultimately, the industrial magnate Werner Siemens personally

The Berlin *Archaeopteryx,* found in 1877 in a limestone quarry near the Bavarian town of Eichstätt. Main slab, left; counterslab, right. (Courtesy of Hermann Jaeger and the Humboldt Museum für Naturkunde, East Berlin.)

paid for the specimen, reselling it to the Prussian Ministry in 1881 for 20,000 deutschemarks. The fossil and counterslab were placed in the Humboldt Museum für Naturkunde.

The Berlin *Archaeopteryx* may well be the most important natural history specimen in existence, perhaps comparable in value to the Rosetta stone. In contrast to the London specimen, the skeleton of the Berlin fossil is articulated in a natural pose with the wings extended. The Berlin specimen is preserved in much the same position as the

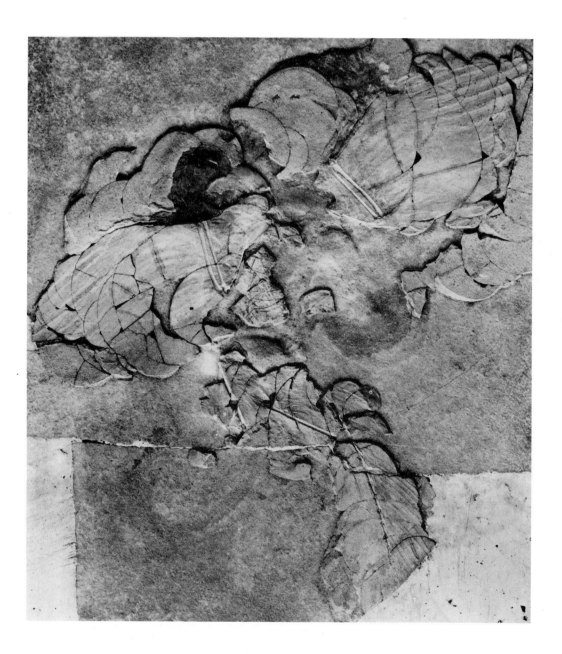

The wings from the counterslab of the Berlin specimen of *Archaeopteryx*. Note the asymmetry of the primary feathers, indicated by the arrows, proving that the wing was aerodynamic. (Courtesy of Hermann Jaeger and the Humboldt Museum für Naturkunde, East Berlin.)

small Solnhofen dinosaur *Compsognathus,* with the head arched back over the neck. The skull, with upper and lower teeth, is complete, and attached to the outspread arms and hands are complete impressions of primary and secondary flight feathers, nearly identical in detail to those of modern birds. The long tail shows a pair of tail feathers attached symmetrically to each vertebra.

At first, scientists thought the Berlin specimen belonged to the same species as the London specimen. But in 1897 Wilhelm Barnim

Dames, the German paleontologist who first described the Berlin fossil, dubbed it *Archaeopteryx siemensii*. Later, in the 1920s, Bronislav Petronievics, greatly overemphasizing the differences between the London and Berlin specimens, named the Berlin bird *Archaeornis siemensii*, placing it in a different genus from *Archaeopteryx* (1925, 1927). He believed that *"Archaeornis"* gave rise to all modern birds except the ostriches and allies, which he thought were descended from the London *Archaeopteryx*. Today, however, most students regard all the

specimens as belonging to the single genus *Archaeopteryx,* but how many fossil species exist is still uncertain.

In 1956 a third skeletal specimen of *Archaeopteryx* was discovered in a quarry shed by a student at the University of Erlangen. The specimen showed some feather impressions, but was so badly disarticulated and, presumably, decomposed that its identification took two years. Finally, Klaus Fesefeldt, a geologist from Erlangen, determined that it was from an area only 250 yards from the site of the recovery of the London specimen. The London specimen, however, had been found in a layer 20 feet lower. For a time the new specimen was placed on public display in a small museum at Maxberg owned by one of the Solnhofen quarry companies, but the original owner recently reclaimed the fossil and it is no longer accessible. Fortunately, John H. Ostrom of Yale University was permitted to study it before it was reclaimed, and was able to determine that some of the bones of the feet, the metatarsals, were partly fused. This anatomical feature presages the condition in modern birds.

The decomposed and disarticulated remains of the Maxberg specimen of *Archaeopteryx,* the third to be discovered. This specimen, found in 1956, clearly shows the metatarsal bones of the foot partly fused, foreshadowing the condition of fused metatarsals in modern birds. (Courtesy of John H. Ostrom and the Peabody Museum of Natural History, Yale University.)

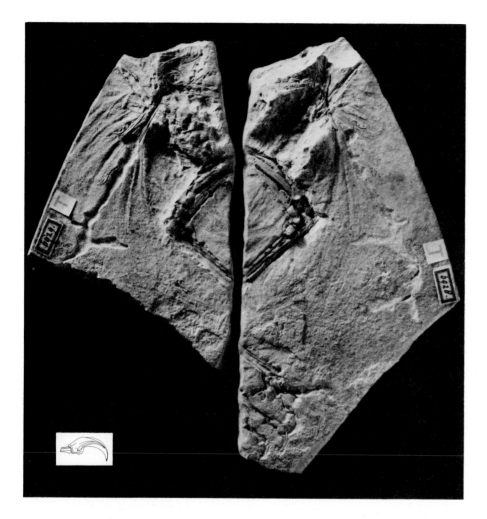

The Teyler specimen of *Archaeopteryx*. Found in 1855, it was long thought to be a pterosaur. Not until 1970 did John H. Ostrom recognize it as a specimen of *Archaeopteryx*. This fossil is particularly interesting because one finger claw is preserved with its horny sheath, as shown in the inset. (Courtesy of John H. Ostrom and the Peabody Museum of Natural History, Yale University.)

In 1970, Ostrom, one of the most astute modern students of dinosaurs, was studying pterodactyls in Europe and happened upon a fourth specimen of *Archaeopteryx* mislabeled as a pterosaur (Ostrom, 1970). The fossil had been recovered in 1855 north of Eichstätt, and had been displayed since 1860 in the Teyler Museum in Haarlem, Netherlands. Amazingly, the Teyler specimen was actually recovered six years before the discovery of the feather and the London specimen, and was announced in 1857 as a flying reptile by none other than Hermann von Meyer, who described it as a new species, *Pterodactylus crassipes.* The Teyler specimen consists of a slab and counterslab that show only faint feather impressions, but very clearly preserve one of the hand claws with its horny sheath.

The story of *Archaeopteryx'* discovery does not end with the Teyler specimen, for in 1973 F. X. Mayr of Eichstätt reported still another specimen of *Archaeopteryx*. This fossil was recovered in 1951 from a quarry a few miles north of Eichstätt and was first identified as the small dinosaur *Compsognathus,* because the feather impressions in the slab were so slight they went unnoticed. Not until 20 years later

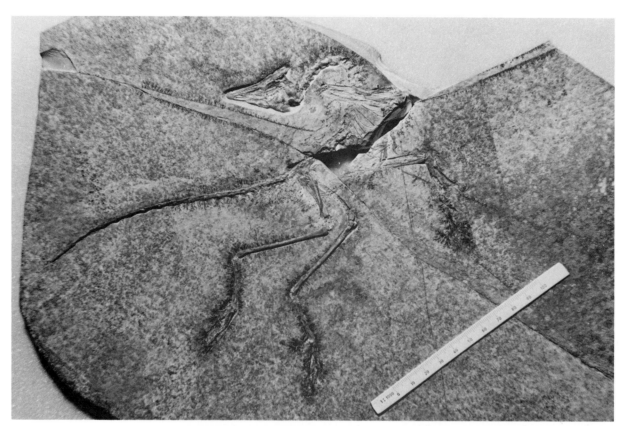

The Eichstätt specimen of *Archaeopteryx*. Unearthed in 1951, it was thought for some 20 years to be the small dinosaur *Compsognathus*. The outline of the wing and tail are very faint. (Courtesy of John H. Ostrom and the Peabody Museum of Natural History, Yale University.)

was the Eichstätt fossil recognized as the fifth specimen of *Archaeopteryx*. It shows exceptionally well-preserved bones with a nearly perfect skull, but the feather impressions are so faint that they are barely discernible as the outline of wings and tail.

Without the presence of feathers, indeed, the bones of the early birds are impossible to separate from those of their reptilian ancestors. As recently as 1978 James Jensen of Brigham Young University announced what he called a possible rival for *Archaeopteryx* from the late Jurassic of Colorado (*Science,* January 1978, p. 284). But the specimen on which he based this claim is a disarticulated femur, and single limb elements from the Jurassic simply cannot be identified with any certainty as avian. There are no skeletal features of *Archaeopteryx*, except the furcula, that are not also found in Jurassic reptiles. In 1881 O. C. Marsh described what he considered to be a Jurassic bird from Wyoming, *Laopteryx prisca,* which turned out to be a pterosaur, and the probability is high that Jensen's "rival" will prove to be the same.

The Ancestry of Birds

2

If *Archaeopteryx* is the oldest known bird, does it necessarily follow that *Archaeopteryx* is ancestral to all subsequent birds? Many authors have argued that *Archaeopteryx* is really a sideline of avian evolution and not on the direct line leading to modern birds. But there is nothing to preclude the possibility that *Archaeopteryx,* if not the actual ancestor, is extremely close to the ancestry of all subsequent birds.

The question that remains, though, is what preceded *Archaeopteryx*? What was the reptilian ancestor from which it descended? Most of the various groups of ruling reptiles of the Mesozoic Era have, at one time or another, been considered the ancestors of birds. After a century of investigation and a fairly satisfactory fossil record of reptiles, the answer remains uncertain. Nonetheless, there are now only two major theories that are widely accepted. They differ with respect to specific lines of descent, and equally important, they differ widely in terms of the time when the first bird appeared.

By tracing the genealogy of reptiles, we can see where the two theories diverge. Ancestral to all other reptilian groups were the stem reptiles, scientifically termed cotylosaurs. The cotylosaurs appeared long before the Age of Reptiles and differed from their descendants in having solid skulls that were not perforated by the openings we call fenestrae.

The next groups we see are the thecodonts, which appeared in early Triassic times, approximately 230 million years ago, and had their own small evolutionary heyday. Thecodonts walked primarily on their hind limbs and were birdlike in many features of the skeleton. They had sharp teeth set in sockets, as in *Archaeopteryx,* and their vertebrae and many other skeletal parts were like those of primitive birds. The first thecodonts were short-legged quadrupeds called the proterosuchians. Emerging quite early in the Triassic Period, they quickly diverged into a number of separate suborders. One of these, the pseudosuchians, is ancestral to all the ruling reptiles, including the dinosaurs; and, through one forebear or another, pseudosuchians gave rise to birds.

It is at this point, in the early Triassic, that proponents of one of the two principal theories place the entry of the first bird. This theory

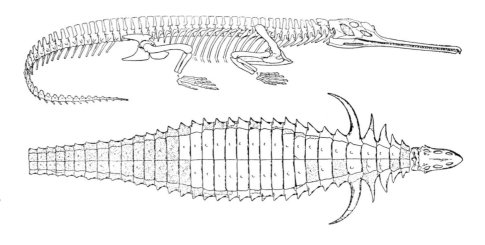

Two forms of the highly divergent quadrupedal thecodonts. The abundant phytosaurs, represented here by *Mystriosuchus* (above), converged on crocodiles in general form, but had the nostrils immediately above the eyes instead of at the tip of the snout. Another bizarre group was the heavily armored aetosaurs, illustrated here by *Desmatosuchus* in dorsal view (below). Both are from the Triassic of North America and were approximately 12 feet long. (From Romer, 1966, © 1933, 1945, and 1966 by The University of Chicago; reprinted by permission of the University of Chicago Press.)

holds that birds descended directly from pseudosuchians about 230 million years ago. The other, competing theory postulates a much later entry of birds into the evolutionary arena after the line of descent had continued through the ruling reptiles, or archosaurs, and through several branching orders of dinosaurs. Before we can compare the two theories, it is necessary to continue our genealogy.

Descended from pseudosuchians, the archosaurs were the dominant reptiles of the Mesozoic Era. Members of this classification, characterized by the presence of two openings in the temporal area of the skull, include a myriad of diverse dinosaurs; the crocodiles, the only surviving group of ruling reptiles and the closest living kin of dinosaurs; and the flying reptiles known as pterosaurs or pterodactyls. Because of their ability to glide, pterosaurs were once considered to be ancestral to birds, but the theory never gained wide acceptance. It is now clear that pterosaurs were at best distant cousins to the birds, but they do provide some interesting evolutionary comparisons.

Pterosaurs originated in the Triassic, millions of years before *Archaeopteryx,* but were predominant only in the latter part of the Mesozoic Era, through the Jurassic to the Cretaceous Period, and went through two waves of evolution in their invasion of the air. Instead of feathers, the pterosaurs depended for flight on a wing membrane, or

A generalized pseudosuchian thecodont (*Hesperosuchus*) from upper Triassic deposits in Arizona. This reptile was slightly over 3 feet long. (Reprinted, by permission, from E. H. Colbert, *Evolution of the Vertebrates,* copyright 1969 by John Wiley & Sons.)

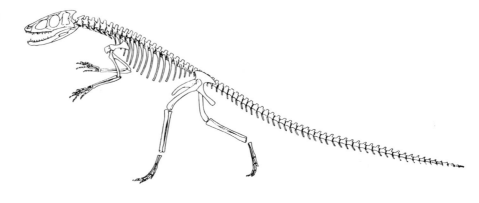

patagium, like that of bats. Being volant, the pterosaurs evolved features that converged on birds in many respects. The skeleton was light in weight and the bones were pneumatic. The sternum was keeled for the attachment of flight muscles that stretched from the keel to an enlarged bony structure on the humerus. The wing bones, though, were highly specialized and different from those of birds. The three inner fingers had short, clawed hooks, possibly used for clinging on sea cliffs; or perhaps pterosaurs hung upside down, in bat fashion.

Almost all pterosaurs are preserved in marine sediments, many laid down in the great epicontinental oceans that covered much of North America in Cretaceous times, and it seems likely that the great majority lived in marine settings. The early pterosaurs had teeth with adaptations indicating that they fed on fish, squid, and similar prey. However, a recently discovered pterosaur from the Cretaceous of Texas lived as far as several hundred miles from the nearest Cretaceous sea. It is tentatively estimated to have had a wing span of up to 50 feet; and with its long neck, it is thought to have been a scavenger, feeding on the carcasses of large dinosaurs.

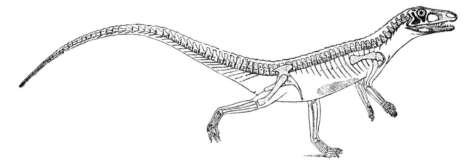

The pseudosuchian thecodont *Ornithosuchus:* (above) restoration of the skeleton; (below) Gerhard Heilmann's life reconstruction. (From Heilmann, 1926.)

Pterosaurs: (*A*) *Ramphorhynchus* of Jurassic age, with a wing spread of about 3 feet; (*B*) *Pteranodon* of Cretaceous age, with a wing spread of about 20 feet. The notarium (fused thoracic vertebrae) served to attach the upper edge of the scapula to the backbone, thus making a strong base for the great wing. Note the loss of the tail and teeth by Cretaceous time and the greatly increased keel on the sternum, which served as the place of attachment for the flight muscles. (Reprinted, by permission, from E. H. Colbert, *Evolution of the Vertebrates,* copyright 1969 by John Wiley & Sons.)

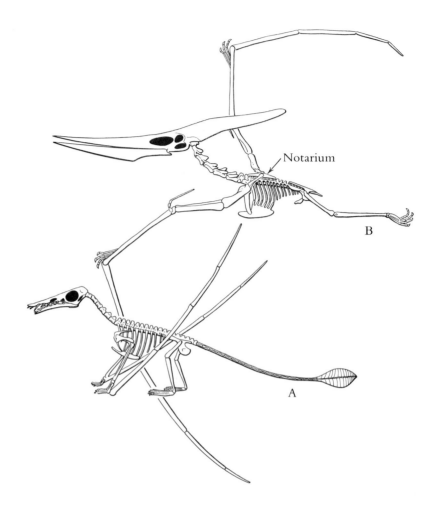

The first evolutionary radiation of pterosaurs produced small to moderate-sized forms with long tails and teeth set in sockets. Many varieties of these tailed pterosaurs are preserved in the Solnhofen lagoons where *Archaeopteryx* lived. The second evolutionary radiation occurred during the Cretaceous, when pterosaurs became very large and, like early birds, lost their teeth and bony tail. By that time, the large *Pteranodon* had attained a wing span of 20 feet, and had a large bony mass projecting backward from its head, which some have thought served as a rudder. Pterosaurs probably depended on sea breezes and associated thermals for soaring. So when the epicontinental seas retreated at the close of the Cretaceous Period, the pterosaurs were doomed to extinction.

The dinosaurs were also doomed, but according to one of our two theories, one of their line managed to give rise to the birds. Very early on, as the chart on page 29 shows, dinosaurs branched into two major groups distinguishable by the structure of their hips: the reptile-hipped saurischians, and the bird-hipped ornithischians. Over the years there has been a strong temptation to try to derive birds from the ornithischians because of this amazing but anatomically superficial re-

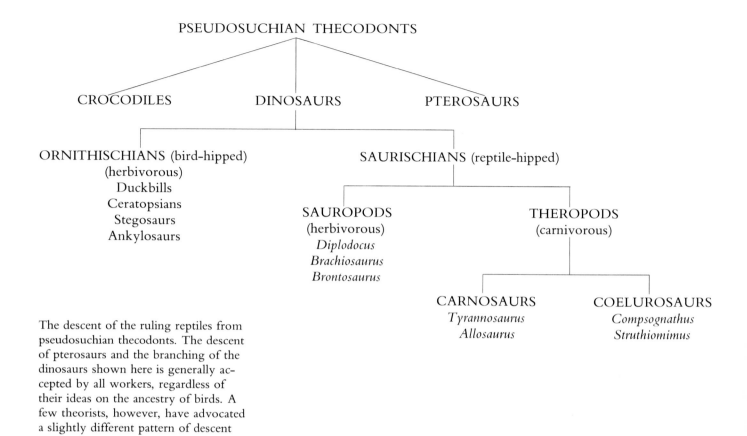

PSEUDOSUCHIAN THECODONTS

CROCODILES   DINOSAURS   PTEROSAURS

ORNITHISCHIANS (bird-hipped)   SAURISCHIANS (reptile-hipped)
(herbivorous)
Duckbills
Ceratopsians   SAUROPODS   THEROPODS
Stegosaurs   (herbivorous)   (carnivorous)
Ankylosaurs   *Diplodocus*
                                Brachiosaurus
                                Brontosaurus
                                              CARNOSAURS   COELUROSAURS
                                              Tyrannosaurus   *Compsognathus*
                                              Allosaurus   *Struthiomimus*

The descent of the ruling reptiles from
pseudosuchian thecodonts. The descent
of pterosaurs and the branching of the
dinosaurs shown here is generally accepted by all workers, regardless of
their ideas on the ancestry of birds. A
few theorists, however, have advocated
a slightly different pattern of descent
for the crocodiles, as we will see later.

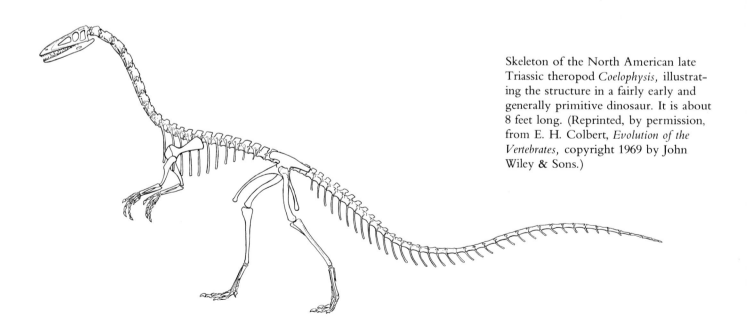

Skeleton of the North American late
Triassic theropod *Coelophysis*, illustrating the structure in a fairly early and
generally primitive dinosaur. It is about
8 feet long. (Reprinted, by permission,
from E. H. Colbert, *Evolution of the
Vertebrates,* copyright 1969 by John
Wiley & Sons.)

Reconstruction of the North American Cretaceous showing several kinds of dinosaurs. On the right is the common aquatic duck-billed dinosaur (hadrosaur) *Edmontosaurus;* in the left background is a herd of the crested duckbill, *Parasaurolophus.* The hooded *Corythosaurus* feeds in the water on the left. The heavily armored ankylosaur *Palaeoscincus* is shown in the center. The only saurischian shown is *Struthiomimus* (background), a coelurosaurian dinosaur remarkably convergent on the living ostrich *Struthio.* (Painting by Charles R. Knight; courtesy of the Field Museum of Natural History, Chicago.)

semblance of the hips. As recently as 1970 Peter M. Galton advocated this view. But ornithischians were highly specialized herbivores and far too removed from the main line to have given rise to any other major group. Their line dead-ended with such forms as the duckbills, the armored ankylosaurs, the plated stegosaurs, and horned ceratopsians like *Triceratops.*

The reptile-hipped saurischians themselves branched into separate herbivorous and carnivorous evolutionary lines. The herbivores, called sauropods, became highly specialized, particularly in adaptations associated with feeding, and many attained gigantic sizes. Giant forms such as *Diplodocus, Brachiosaurus,* and *Brontosaurus* are among the favorites of museum-goers, but that is where their story ends. It is the carnivorous line of saurischians, called theropods, that continues the theoretical lineage toward the birds.

Two groups of theropods emerged, distinguishable by size. The larger group, called carnosaurs, led, once again, to prized museum pieces—*Tyrannosaurus* and *Allosaurus.* The smaller group, however, termed coelurosaurs, included *Struthiomimus,* a Cretaceous dinosaur convergent on living ostriches, and the smallest known dinosaur, the chicken-sized *Compsognathus,* previously encountered in the upper Jurassic Solnhofen limestone.

As you recall, Thomas Huxley found the resemblance between *Compsognathus* and *Archaeopteryx* very telling: "Surely there is nothing very wild or illegitimate in the hypothesis that the phylum of the Class of Aves has its foot in the Dinosaurian Reptiles—that these, passing through a series of such modifications as are exhibited in one of their phases by *Compsognathus,* have given rise to [birds]" (1868, p. 74). Thus was born the theory that birds originated from coelurosaurian dinosaurs.

Huxley's contemporary Benjamin Mudge, of the University of Kansas, among others, found the dinosaurs far too diverse and highly specialized to have been the progenitors of birds: "The dinosaurs vary so much from each other that it is difficult to give a single trait that runs through the whole. But no single genus or set of genera have many features in common with the birds, or a single persistent, typical element or structure which is found in both" (1879, p. 226).

The world's largest mounted dinosaur, the late Jurassic sauropod *Brachiosaurus.* It was 70 feet long, 40 feet tall from feet to skull, and is estimated to have weighed 80 or 90 tons. This specimen, the only complete skeleton in existence, was discovered in Tanzania by a German expedition under the direction of W. Janensch, and was excavated at the famous Tendaguru site, which produced thousands of dinosaur bones between 1909 and 1912. It is exhibited in the Museum für Naturkunde in East Berlin, and is shown here with a human skeleton at its feet. A skeleton of a dinosaur similar to the sauropod *Diplodocus* stands mounted in the background. Recently, James Jensen has collected some bones of a dinosaur from the upper Jurassic deposits of Colorado's Dry Mesa Quarry that may have been one-fifth larger than *Brachiosaurus;* it has been provisionally termed "Supersaurus"; if it did indeed resemble *Brachiosaurus,* it would have towered to 50 feet and weighed as much as 100 tons, or approximately fifteen times as much as an adult African bull elephant. (Courtesy of Hermann Jaeger and the Humboldt Museum für Naturkunde, East Berlin.)

Heilmann's reconstructions of gorgo-
saurs (carnosaurs) at the carcass of a
duckbill dinosaur (*Trachodon*) and of
Struthiomimus, a coelurosaurian dinosaur
convergent on living ostriches. (From
Heilmann, 1926.)

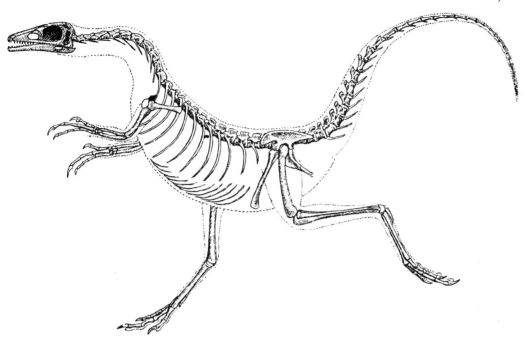

Heilmann's reconstruction of the skeleton and living coelurosaur *Compsognathus longipes,* from the upper Jurassic Solnhofen limestone. (From Heilmann, 1926.)

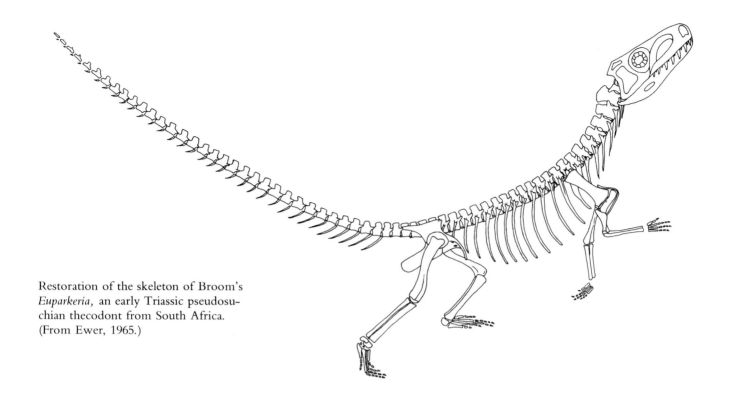

Restoration of the skeleton of Broom's *Euparkeria*, an early Triassic pseudosuchian thecodont from South Africa. (From Ewer, 1965.)

The debate continued, but the arguments began to shift when Robert Broom, a prominent South African paleontologist, first proposed what has come to be known as the pseudosuchian thecodont theory. In 1913 Broom described from the rich lower Triassic deposits of South Africa a fossil, *Euparkeria,* that he believed was ancestral not only to birds, but also to the ruling reptiles:

> There cannot, I think, be the slightest doubt that the Pseudosuchia have close affinities with the Dinosaurs, or at least with the Theropoda. This has been recognized by Marsh, v. Huene and others. In fact there seems to me little doubt that the ancestral Dinosaur was a Pseudosuchian . . . There is still another group for which some Pseudosuchian has probably been ancestral, namely the Birds. For a time one or other of the Dinosaurs was regarded as near the avian ancestor . . . Seven years ago . . . I argued that the bird had come from the groups immediately ancestral to the Theropodous Dinosaurs. The Pseudosuchia, now that it is better known, proves to be just such a group as is required. In those points where we find the Dinosaur too specialized, we see the Pseudosuchian still primitive enough.   (1913, p. 631)

Euparkeria, this small, bipedal pseudosuchian 230 million years old, appeared to have all the necessary anatomical qualifications to be the ancestor of birds. No longer was it necessary to deal with the problem of dinosaurian specialization.

Thus when the distinguished Danish paleontologist Gerhard Heilmann wrote the first major book on avian evolution, *The Origin of*

Birds (1926), he considered Broom's *Euparkeria* the key to avian ancestry. Heilmann meticulously described how *Archaeopteryx* could have arisen from *Euparkeria* and how flight could have evolved from small bipedal reptiles. But his argument works equally well to validate a much later descent from a small coelurosaurian dinosaur. Indeed, Heilmann himself seems to have had misgivings; he found many similarities between *Archaeopteryx* and the small coelurosaurian dinosaurs, just as Huxley had. His ambivalence permeates the book, but in the end he argued for early pseudosuchian ancestry:

> It would seem a rather obvious conclusion that it is amongst the coelurosaurs that we are to look for the bird ancestor. And yet, this would be too rash, for the very fact that clavicles are wanting would in itself be sufficient to prove that these saurians could not possibly be the ancestors of birds . . . We have therefore reasons to hope that in a group of reptiles closely related to the coelurosaurs we shall be able to find an animal wholly without the shortcomings here indicated for bird ancestors . . . such a group is possibly the pseudosuchians . . . All our requirements of a bird ancestor are met in the pseudosuchians, and nothing in their structure militates against the view that one of them might have been the ancestor of the birds.   (1926, pp. 183–185)

Heilmann's *Origin of Birds* was engaging and well documented; it had all the earmarks of authority. It also had a lasting influence. For the next fifty years, although some authors proposed alternative theories, Heilmann's early pseudosuchian thecodont ancestor was supported in virtually every subsequent textbook and paper on avian origins. Even within the last decade, Alick D. Walker of Newcastle University (1972, 1977) proposed a variation on Heilmann's theory: that both birds and crocodiles arose in the Triassic from a common pseudosuchian thecodont ancestor somewhat more specialized than Broom's *Euparkeria*. Walker derived his theory from the morphology of *Sphenosuchus,* a primitive, probably arboreal relative of crocodiles from the late Triassic of South Africa.

But what about the element of time? *Euparkeria* is from the early Triassic, approximately 230 million years ago, and *Sphenosuchus* from the late Triassic, 200 million years ago. *Archaeopteryx,* not far removed structurally from reptilian anatomy, is from the late Jurassic, 140 million years ago. So a vast gap would exist between ancestor and descendant. This problem is not impossible to overcome, for there could have been later pseudosuchians and earlier birds, but the pseudosuchians were such generalized animals that in the intervening millennia they could have given rise to any number of diverse groups. The evolutionist would hope to find a more immediate ancestor for birds, one removed from the thecodonts, but not so highly specialized that it could not be ancestral to birds. Such an ancestor should share some specialized features with *Archaeopteryx* itself.

Skulls of: (*A*) the pseudosuchian thecodont *Euparkeria*; (*B*) the coelurosaurian dinosaur *Compsognathus*; (*C*) *Archaeopteryx*; and (*D*) a modern pigeon, *Columba*. (Drawing by Sigrid K. James.)

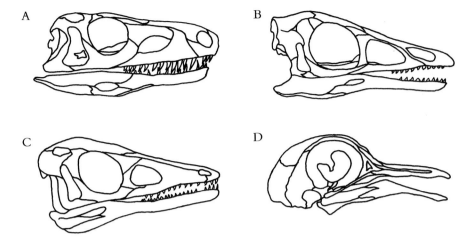

Not long after correctly identifying the Teyler specimen of *Archaeopteryx* in 1970, John H. Ostrom began a line of research that led him to the conclusion, originally propounded by Huxley in 1868, that birds are derived from the small theropod dinosaurs called coelurosaurians. As Ostrom points out:

> It has been repeatedly observed that the *Archaeopteryx* specimens are very birdlike, but also possess a number of reptilian features . . . the actual fact is that these specimens are not particularly like *modern* birds at all. If feather impressions had not been preserved in the London and Berlin specimens, they never would have been identified as birds. Instead, they would unquestionably have been labelled as coelurosaurian dinosaurs . . . the last three specimens [of *Archaeopteryx*] to be recognized were all misidentified at first, and the Eichstätt specimen for twenty years was thought to be a small specimen of the dinosaur *Compsognathus*. (1975, p. 61)

In recent years, Ostrom has built a strong argument for the coelurosaurian dinosaur origin of birds backed by a mass of documentation. Ostrom shows that many of the more specialized anatomical features found in *Archaeopteryx* also characterize theropod dinosaurs, and represent advancements over the thecodonts. Except for the uniquely avian fused clavicles that form the furcula, every feature of the skeletal structure of *Archaeopteryx* can be found in more than one of the coelurosaurs. These anatomical characteristics include the structure of the vertebral column, peculiarities of the forelimbs, the proportions of bones in the hand, the form of the humerus and the ulna, the pectoral arch, the hind limb, and the pelvis. Ostrom concludes that the *only* bony feature of *Archaeopteryx* that is exclusively avian is the furcula. The critical question then becomes, in Ostrom's words,

> Is it more probable that *Archaeopteryx* acquired the large number of derived [unique] "theropod" characters by convergence or in parallel at the same time that these same features were being ac-

quired by some coelurosaurian theropods—presumably from a common ancestor? Or is it more likely that these many derived characters are common to some small theropods and *Archaeopteryx* because *Archaeopteryx* evolved directly from such a theropod? . . . there is absolutely no question in my mind that the last explanation is far more probable. (1975, p. 74)

In addition to the many anatomical characteristics shared by theropod dinosaurs and birds, the appearance of both in the same geologic period lends credence to a dinosaurian ancestry. After all, there is a gap of some 90 million years between the thecodont *Euparkeria* and *Archaeopteryx,* but small coelurosaurian dinosaurs such as *Compsognathus* occur in the same Solnhofen limestone from which *Archaeopteryx* was recovered. Coelurosaurs, however, are principally a Cretaceous group, with few forms extending back into the Jurassic; and one problem with Ostrom's theory is that most of his comparisons of unique characters shared by *Archaeopteryx* and coelurosaurs are made with dinosaur species from the late Cretaceous that lived after *Archaeopteryx.*

Nonetheless, it appeared until very recently that a dinosaurian ancestry of *Archaeopteryx* would stand as the most acceptable and simplest theory for the origin of birds. The evolutionary sequence would go from pseudosuchian thecodonts to a theropod, coelurosaurian dinosaur to *Archaeopteryx* and eventually to modern birds. In 1979, however, K. N. Whetstone and Larry D. Martin published a paper that supports Walker's *Sphenosuchus* hypothesis and casts considerable doubt once again on the Huxley-Ostrom theory of dinosaurian ancestry. Whetstone and Martin's evidence, based on the structure of the ear, strongly supports the view that birds and crocodiles originated from a shared pseudosuchian ancestor before the advent of either ornithischian or saurischian dinosaurs. They show that peculiar ear sinuses are found in Mesozoic birds such as *Hesperornis* and in Triassic crocodilians such as *Notochampsa,* but not in theropod dinosaurs. They conclude that "a theory of a pseudosuchian origin for birds is, at the very least, a reasonable alternative to the dinosaur model proposed by Ostrom" (1979, p. 236).

On the evidence available so far, it is difficult to choose between the dinosaurian and pseudosuchian theories of avian ancestry. Both have much to recommend them, but perhaps an early, generalized pseudosuchian is a slightly better candidate. The time gap between birds and pseudosuchians seems easier to accept than coelurosaurian ancestors that, except for a few forms like *Compsognathus,* mostly postdated *Archaeopteryx.* However, while *Euparkeria* is sufficiently generalized to be the forebear, Walker's *Sphenosuchus* seems slightly too specialized to fill the bill, though perhaps a forerunner of this crocodilelike creature was the shared ancestor of birds and crocodiles.

Another point favoring the early pseudosuchian theory is the evolution of the elongated forelimbs seen in *Archaeopteryx* and typical of birds. As we will see later, birds originated in the trees. The coelurosaurs had already attained the erect posture and greatly reduced forelimbs suggestive of terrestrial rather than arboreal locomotion, although these small dinosaurs were probably quite versatile in their behavior. Many pseudosuchians, however, had not yet become fully erect and were no doubt quite arboreal, showing little reduction in their forelimbs. Such forms could easily have evolved the elongation of the forelimbs seen in *Archaeopteryx,* but for coelurosaurs to develop lengthened forelimbs from their already reduced and somewhat vestigial hands would demand a drastic reversal in evolution. Moreover, as we shall see in Chapter 3, *Archaeopteryx* was well on its way to being a real bird and could well be the descendant of some form intermediate between reptiles and birds that occurred much earlier than coelurosaurs.

The Evolution of Flight

3

When they began to fly, birds either lifted themselves up from the ground or glided down from high places; it is difficult to imagine a third alternative. In either case, the anatomical changes needed for flying must have evolved in a sequence of very small steps, because nothing we know about evolution allows us to believe that feathered wings could have appeared abruptly as an innovation in avian anatomy. Wings must have evolved over a very long time span. And each new modification of body plan or limbs during that period must have made some contribution to fitness long before the day when a jumping or gliding creature gave the first strong beat of its forelimbs and ceased simply falling back to earth.

So, to reconstruct the evolution of modern birds, we must account for the sequence of changes that converted reptilian scales into feathers and, along the way, we must answer certain questions: Were the reptilian ancestors of birds jumpers or gliders? Was *Archaeopteryx* itself at home on the ground or in trees? Could it only glide or did it already have the ability to sustain flight? What was the original advantage of feathers or their precursors?

Before speculating about how flight originated in birds, we should consider other large animals that have taken to the air. All other flying or gliding vertebrates began their evolution in trees, with the possible exception of the pterosaurs, which may have begun flying by gliding out from sea cliffs. As a general rule, then, beginning fliers use the energy that gravity provides: they climb up and coast down. They do not start their flight by expending the burst of effort needed to rise off the ground.

Several kinds of reptile or amphibian have achieved periods of airborne existence one way or another. An early example was the Triassic dawn lizards, related to the precursors of true lizards (which, like birds, appeared in the late Jurassic Period). Some dawn lizards developed a pair of horizontal sails in which a modified set of ribs grew straight out to form struts lying in a horizontal plane instead of curving around to enclose the chest. The skin stretched over these ribs provided a sail surface, and this allowed the animal to volplane from tree to tree.

A group of extant lizards, at a much later time, also acquired the art of gliding. Living in trees of the Malay Peninsula and islands of the western Pacific, these so-called flying dragons number some two dozen species of the genus *Draco*. The flight structure of these lizards is a membrane, or patagium, stretched between the forelimb and hind limb that is stiffened by six very long ribs, somewhat in the manner of the dawn lizards. Although this equipment seems meager, *Draco* lizards are highly maneuverable and can steer well enough to select a landing site on a particular tree.

Not only lizards but tree-dwelling snakes have developed adaptations permitting them some travel time in the air. Members of the snake genus *Chrysopela* engage in a kind of parachuting. When they fall from a tree, they pull in their abdomens and thus flatten their bodies so that they sail rather than drop to a lower point. And an amphibian, the parachuting Malay frog *Rhacophorus*, accomplishes much the same end by extending its limbs, which support broad flaps of skin, and its long, fully webbed toes. Although these parachuting forms have little steering ability, they are at least able to check the full impact of their fall, and the ability is clearly adaptive: the animal can quickly escape from predators, is protected from injury if it falls accidentally, and perhaps can pursue its prey by this means.

Among mammals, only the bats have developed true flight. Derived from arboreal insectivores, bats have formed their wing from a membrane stretched between their skeletal "fingers" and their hind appendage. A number of other mammals have become highly competent gliders, including the flying squirrels, the flying lemurs (or colugos), and, representing the marsupials, the flying phalangers. These animals are able to select a tree trunk at a great distance from their point of takeoff, steer accurately through the intervening air, and maneuver as necessary before striking the tree.

All of these vertebrate forms, living or extinct, parachuting, gliding, or truly flying, share one feature in common: an arboreal origin. None of them began flying from a purely ground-dwelling habit. This fact alone argues strongly against the theory that birds began as runners and jumpers. Yet some have advocated the cursorial theory (from the Latin *cursus,* past participle of *run*) to explain the origin of flight.

First to propose a cursorial origin of flight was Samuel Wendell Williston, a foremost expert on fossil reptiles and a dinosaur collector for O. C. Marsh. "It is not difficult," Williston wrote in 1879, "to understand how the forelegs of a dinosaur might have been changed to wings. During the great extent of time in the Triassic, for which we have scanty records, there may have been a gradual lengthening of the outer fingers and greater development of the scales, thus aiding the animal in running. The further change to feathers would have been easy. The wings must first have been used in running, next in leaping and descending from heights, and finally in soaring" (p. 459).

Baron Nopsca's hypothetical reconstruction of a running proavis. (Drawing by Sigrid K. James, after Nopsca, 1907.)

Williston's rather casual hypothesis enjoyed little support among his contemporaries. The following year, O. C. Marsh proposed, apparently for the first time, an arboreal theory: "The power of flight probably originated among small arboreal forms of reptilian birds. How this may have commenced, we have an indication in the flight of *Galeopithecus,* the flying squirrels (*Pteromys*), the flying lizards (*Draco*) and the flying tree frog (*Rhacophorus*). In the early arboreal birds, which jumped from branch to branch, even rudimentary feathers on the fore limbs would be an advantage as they would tend to lengthen a downward leap or break the force of a fall" (1880, p. 189). The arboreal theory has recruited the majority of adherents since then, but the cursorial alternative has had at least two significant revivals in the last hundred years.

One of these was offered in 1907, by a flamboyant self-trained Transylvanian paleontologist, Baron Francis Nopsca, whose biography includes spying in World War I, volunteering his services as heir-designate to the vacant Albanian throne, murdering his homosexual lover, and then killing himself. Many of Nopsca's ideas were as colorful as his life. He envisioned the predecessors of birds as long-tailed reptiles that flapped their forelimbs while running across the ground. The reptilian scales on their forearms became elongated in the process, and their hind margins eventually sprouted feathers. In a paper entitled "Ideas on the Origin of Flight," Nopsca wrote:

> We may quite well suppose that birds originated from bipedal long-tailed cursorial reptiles which during running oared along in the air by flapping their free anterior extremities.
>
> By gradually increasing in size, the enlarged but perhaps horny hypothetical scales of the antibrachial [forearm area] margin would in time enable the yet carnivorous and cursorial ancestor of Birds to take long strides and leaps much in the same manner of the domesticated Goose or Storks when starting, and ultimately develop to actual feathers; this epidermic cover would also raise the temperature of the body, and thus help to increase the mental and bodily activities of these rapacious forms. (1907, p. 234)

The double-crested basilisk (*Basiliscus plumbifrons*), a tropical American lizard that can rear up and run on its hind legs in a semierect manner. Versatile tree-climbers, basilisks have special adaptations of the feet that permit them to run over the surface of water for short distances. Nopsca thought that a quadruped much like the basilisk was the first step in the transition from reptiles to birds. (New York Zoological Society Photo.)

Turning specifically to *Archaeopteryx,* Nopsca reckoned that the fossil creature, though not an accomplished flier, was quite far removed from the early stages leading to flight: "The rounded contour of the *Archaeopteryx* wing, together with the feebly developed sternum, show us that *Archaeopteryx,* though perhaps not an altogether badly flying creature, can on no account have been a soaring bird, but a bird that was yet in the first stage of active flight" (1907, p. 16).

In Nopsca's scenario, the transition from reptiles to birds began with a primitive, quadrupedal animal that could rise up to run on its hind legs, as do the living double-crested lizards, *Basiliscus,* of Central America or the frilled lizards, *Chlamydosaurus,* of Australia. These animals then became obligatory bipeds, such as the small dinosaur *Compsognathus,* and from them the forebears of the birds arose.

Nopsca's theory was undermined by its aerodynamic absurdity. Imagine the incredible energy that his creature must expend to get airborne. Once aloft, where would it find the power to stay in flight? The main thrust, which, in Nopsca's conception, came from the traction of the hind feet on the ground, would have disappeared. It is highly unlikely that the flapping forearm propellors Nopsca imagined would have sufficed to keep the bird from crashing promptly back to earth.

Nearly a hundred years after Williston advanced the first cursorial theory, John H. Ostrom proposed a very different version of it. Unlike its predecessors, Ostrom's theory has been very widely accepted, and his view of *Archaeopteryx* as a nonflying reptile is found in many textbooks.

Ostrom reasoned from features of *Archaeopteryx* anatomy and from features of dinosaurs contemporary with it. Along with some other paleontologists, he believes that "warm-bloodedness," or endothermy, first evolved among dinosaurs. The first feathers, in this scheme, served certain groups of dinosaurs as a thermoregulatory pelt. Accordingly, the small theropod dinosaurs that *Archaeopteryx* anatomically resembles—the coelurosaurians—would have been warm-blooded animals, and the first feathers covered them not as aids to flight but as insulating material. The head and mouth of *Archaeopteryx,* Ostrom argues, indicate that it preyed on relatively small animals, such as insects, lizards, and small mammals. Running after such creatures on its two hind legs, *Archaeopteryx* used its forelimbs to catch them. In time, elongation of the forelimb feathers made them more efficient for trapping prey. They became a kind of butterfly net that *Archaeopteryx* used to corral its supper.

In this account of *Archaeopteryx'* evolution, the feathers that first served for thermoregulation acquired a second, unrelated function when they began helping to trap prey. This was an instance of preadaptation: a structure evolved for one specific function (insulation) acquired a form that made it easy to assume a second, biologically unrelated one (insect trapping). Subsequently, the elongated feathers, by providing lift to the animal during running and leaping, began to serve the purpose of flight, again a case of preadaptation. As Ostrom summarizes:

> It is my contention that *Archaeopteryx* was not especially arboreal in its habits, but rather was a very active, fleet-footed, bipedal, cursorial predator in which the hands, arms, and pectoral arch were primarily for seizing and holding small prey, as was almost certainly the situation in *Ornitholestes, Velociraptor, Deinonychus* and other small theropods . . . I suggest that it was the prior release of the forelimb from normal terrestrial locomotion (probably for purposes of predation) and its modification into an elongated, predatory, grasping appendage with *strong powers of abduction* that pre-adapted the forelimb as a "proto-wing." (1974, p. 34)

Ostrom continues the argument as follows:

> If vigorous flapping of the feathered forelimbs played a part at any stage in the business of catching prey, the increased surface area of the enlarged contour feathers would undoubtedly have produced some lift during such assaults. From this point, it is a small evolutionary step for selection to improve those features that were important for flapping, leaping attacks on prey—perhaps to "fly up" after escaping insects: e.g., enlargement of the primaries and secondaries and their firm, rigid attachment to the forelimb skeleton; elongation and specialization of the bones of the forelimb and hand; retention of the theropodlike scapula and coracoids; enlargement of the pectoral abductor muscles; and stabilization of the shoulder joints by fusion of the clavicle . . . Thus, selection would tend to improve not only the "flight power," but also the "flight controls"—the associated sensory and motor neural components. (1974, p. 35)

Ostrom discounts certain features of *Archaeopteryx'* anatomy that suggest that the animal was arboreal, not ground-dwelling, for instance, the hind toe, or hallux. In *Archaeopteryx* the hallux is turned backward, as in all modern birds. This is an adaptation that characterizes animals that make their way through trees; it helps them grasp the branches. Ostrom, however, interprets the feature differently (1974).

Ostrom's widely accepted cursorial predator theory for *Archaeopteryx* envisions it as a small terrestrial theropod dinosaur using its wings as an insect trap. (Drawing by Sigrid K. James.)

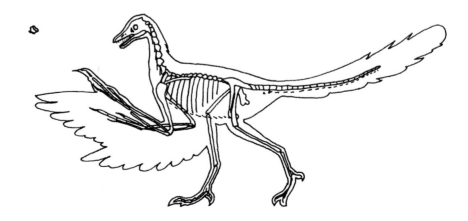

Noting that the backward-directed toe "apparently was present in all carnivorous theropods, but never existed in equally bipedal but herbivorous ornithopods," he concludes that the original function of the reversed toe was related not to climbing, but to diet. The foot with the backward-directed toe was useful in capturing prey.

Ostrom's theory also fails to take account of other avian characteristics of *Archaeopteryx,* and this may be its fatal flaw. He repeatedly emphasizes the fossil's lack of birdlike features and reiterates the old argument that, were it not for the presence of feathers, the fossil would surely have been classified as a small dinosaur. But this interpretation neglects two distinctly avian traits of *Archaeopteryx* that indicate it could fly. One is feathers, which have not in fact been found in dinosaur fossils and which have characteristics suggesting that they were aerodynamically effective. The other is the furcula, a structure that is hard to explain except as an aid to flight.

A theory that contradicts none of the evidence from either *Archaeopteryx* or other fossil finds is the arboreal hypothesis that Marsh had first sketched out in 1880. Marsh's views were rather widely accepted by other students of avian evolution and have subsequently been elaborated. C. H. Hurst, a paleontologist interested in fossil reptiles, was intrigued by the long-clawed fingers of *Archaeopteryx* and proposed in 1893 that they could have been used for climbing in trees. A year later, William Plane Pycraft, a distinguished English ornithologist, suggested that claws would be useful only to nestlings, which would need them for climbing back to the nest in the event of an unlucky fall. Pycraft drew an analogy with the hoatzin (*Opisthocomus hoazin*), a strange South American bird that nests gregariously in bushes overhanging streams of the Amazon basin. The young of this species have well-developed claws on both the first and second digits; soon after hatching, they use their claws to climb about the nest and nearby branches. When threatened with danger, the young birds fling themselves into the water and then use the claws to climb back to their nest. At the time Pycraft wrote his paper (1894), the hoatzin's claws were thought to be a primitive feature retained from *Archaeopteryx.* Now, however, it is generally believed that the hoatzin's claws evolved secondarily.

Nevertheless, the young hoatzin's claws may well be analogous to some stage in evolution preceding *Archaeopteryx.* For although *Achaeopteryx* had well-developed flight feathers, as we shall see, with its wings folded the animal could have used its claws as an aid in climbing, and it is not difficult to imagine the young *Archaeopteryx* or other primitive fledglings using their claws like a hoatzin. It is also possible that the three-clawed fingers of *Archaeopteryx* aided flight as well as climbing. They might have acted as a primitive mid-wing slot, comparable to the alula, or bastard wing, located at the same position in modern birds.

A baby hoatzin using its claws to climb back up to the nest; the adult hoatzin is shown in silhouette. (Drawings by Sigrid K. James, after Austin, 1961.)

The left hand of a hoatzin embryo
(above) compared with that of the
adult (below). (From Heilmann, 1926.)

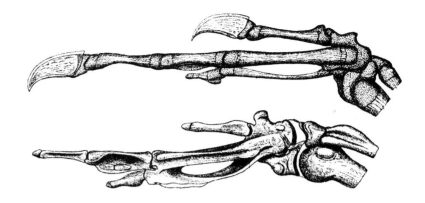

Dorsal views of the left hand of *Archaeopteryx* (left), a nestling hoatzin
(center), and a young pigeon (right).
(From Heilmann, 1926.)

The arboreal theory was tremendously bolstered in 1926 by Gerhard Heilmann in *The Origin of Birds.* There Heilmann reconstructed in convincing detail the hypothetical stages of evolution from terrestrial to tree-dwelling to flying animal. But he did not pay much attention to the adaptive advantage of each microevolutionary step that eventually led to the macroevolutionary change from reptile to bird. More recently (1965), Walter Bock of Columbia University has carefully analyzed the arboreal theory and identified the adaptive purpose of each intermediate stage; he shows vividly that the arboreal theory is compatible with the principles of microevolution. Bock's model is in harmony with the preference of modern theorists for evolutionary pathways that follow simple, direct routes without elaborate intermediate steps.

A hypothetical proavis using its claws to climb up a tree trunk. (Drawing by Sigrid K. James.)

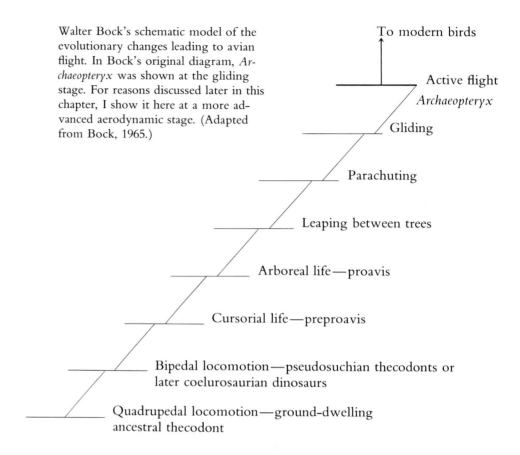

Walter Bock's schematic model of the evolutionary changes leading to avian flight. In Bock's original diagram, *Archaeopteryx* was shown at the gliding stage. For reasons discussed later in this chapter, I show it here at a more advanced aerodynamic stage. (Adapted from Bock, 1965.)

To modern birds

Active flight
Archaeopteryx

Gliding

Parachuting

Leaping between trees

Arboreal life—proavis

Cursorial life—preproavis

Bipedal locomotion—pseudosuchian thecodonts or later coelurosaurian dinosaurs

Quadrupedal locomotion—ground-dwelling ancestral thecodont

In Bock's version of the arboreal theory, a four-footed, ground-dwelling reptile is the ancestral form. It became bipedal, then took to climbing and the arboreal life, then began leaping from tree to tree. And from there it expanded its repertoire to include parachuting, gliding, and, finally, active, powered flight. This sequence of events, fully adaptive at each stage, led not only from quadrupedal ambulation to powered flight, but from reptile to bird.

As for *Archaeopteryx,* it and other hypothetical proto-birds have usually been thought of as either entirely ground-dwelling or entirely arboreal, but there is no reason why they could not have been both. In living reptiles such as the Central American basilisk and in living birds we find species capable of ground-dwelling and arboreal activity. And in its skeletal proportions, *Archaeopteryx* is quite similar to the living touracos (Musophagidae) and chachalacas (Cracidae), birds that are both arboreal and terrestrial and capable of a myriad of behaviors. *Archaeopteryx* may well have been at home both on the ground and in trees, and could well have been capable of climbing. Perhaps Pierce Brodkorb of the University of Florida has best summarized its probable behavioral repertoire:

Without question *Archaeopteryx* had arboreal habits similar to those of the Cracidae and Musophagidae. It probably used its clawed fingers to cling to twigs in the manner of young hoatzins. It may have come down to drink, as do the cracids (guans) . . . but the long flat tail was not that of a ground dweller or a water bird. Its soft, wide rectrices soon would become frayed on the ground or sodden in the water . . . Like the touracos . . . *Archaeopteryx* probably ran agilely along the branches, leaping from perch to perch, and swooping from tree to tree. Its flight must have been uncertain and probably consisted of a combination of gliding and flapping, with the tail used both for support and for steering.   (1971, p. 34)

The wings that sustained *Archaeopteryx'* combination of flapping and gliding closely resemble, in their basic design, those of many arboreal, perching birds. Almost perfectly preserved in the Berlin specimen, the wings have the outline of an aerodynamic, elliptical structure. As Josselyn Van Tyne and Andrew J. Berger point out, the elliptical wing is "characterized by a low aspect ratio and only a slight amount of wing-tip vortex. This type [of wing] is found in birds which 'must move easily through restricted openings in vegetation:

A hypothetical proavis gliding from tree to tree. (Drawing by Sigrid K. James.)

gallinaceous birds, doves, woodcocks, woodpeckers, and most passerine birds'" (1976, p. 383). The aerodynamic wing of birds, a design that modern aircraft improve on only in detail, provides good lift and offers great maneuverability. The only feature of modern birds missing from the wing of *Archaeopteryx* is the mid-wing slot.

The basic pattern of the wing feathers in *Archaeopteryx* was also essentially that of modern birds. In the Berlin specimen there are 9 primaries (modern birds have 9 to 12), and the first 3 are reduced in length progressively inward, as they are in many modern birds. Likewise, *Archaeopteryx* has 14 secondaries, well within the range of 7 to 32 that characterizes modern birds.

Were the feathers themselves designed for flight? In any feather of modern birds, the long, tapered central shaft, called the rachis, supports the interlocking microscopic barbs that form a sheet on either

Heilmann's reconstruction of the outstretched wing of *Archaeopteryx* in dorsal view (above) and ventral view (below). The insert illustrates the position of the claws. (From Heilmann, 1926.)

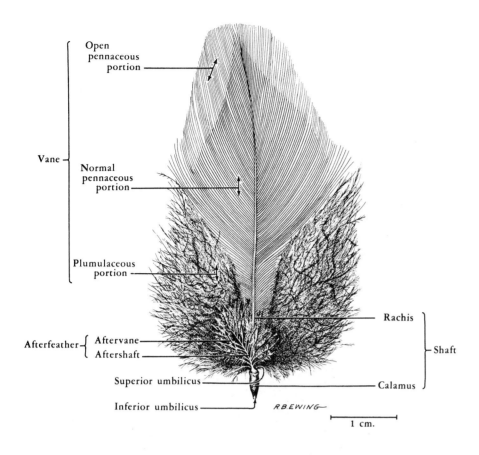

Open
pennaceous
portion

Vane

Normal
pennaceous
portion

Plumulaceous
portion

Rachis

Afterfeather { Aftervane
Aftershaft

Shaft

Superior umbilicus

Calamus

Inferior umbilicus

R.B EWING

1 cm.

Main parts of a typical contour feather, exemplified by a feather from the middle of the back of a domestic chicken. (From Lucas and Stettenheim, 1972; courtesy of Alfred M. Lucas.)

Feathers of the domestic chicken: (left) contour feather with small aftershaft from the breast region; (right) primary wing feather. Note the symmetry of the vanes in the breast feather and the asymmetric vanes in the flight feather. The leading edge of the flight feather, the smaller vane, is in direct contact with the air in flight. (From Lucas and Stettenheim, 1972; courtesy of Alfred M. Lucas.)

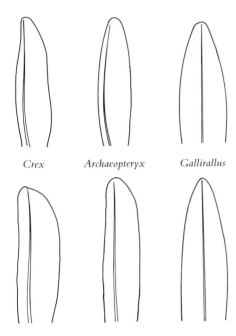

Crex   *Archaeopteryx*   *Gallirallus*

Flight feathers from the left wings of *Crex crex* (a flying rail), *Archaeopteryx,* and *Gallirallus australis* (a flightless rail): (above) distal ends of the second primaries (counting inward); (below) distal ends of the sixth primaries. All are drawn to scale. (From Feduccia and Tordoff, *Science,* 203:1021–1022, March 1979; drawing by Ellen Paige; copyright 1979 by the American Association for the Advancement of Science.)

side, called the vane. The contour, or body, feathers have symmetrical or nearly symmetrical vanes. But strongly asymmetric vanes appear in the flight feathers; the asymmetry is most marked in the primaries, somewhat less pronounced in the secondaries, and is present in all the tail feathers except the central pair. In all asymmetric feathers the rachis lies toward the leading edge of the feather, which is thicker, stiffer, and narrower than the trailing vane. As a result of their asymmetry, flight feathers have an airfoil cross section. In most birds the outer primaries function as individual airfoils to produce lift during flapping flight. In the strongest fliers, such as hawks, swifts, and hummingbirds, the asymmetry is most pronounced. The short, stiffened vanes on the leading edge of feathers in the inner wing and tail contribute stability to the overall aerodynamic design.

In short, the presence of asymmetry in feathers argues that they are used for flight, a generalization confirmed by evidence from birds that have given up flying. The flightless ostriches (*Struthio*) and South American rheas (*Rhea* and *Pterocnemia*) descended from flying birds, but their wing and flight feathers remain only for display, perhaps for thermoregulation, and for balance in running. In these birds the vanes of the primary feathers are symmetrical. In birds that have become flightless more recently, such as the flightless rails on islands of the South Pacific (especially the genera *Atlantisia* and *Gallirallus*), the symmetry is strikingly perfect (Feduccia and Tordoff, 1979).

But what of *Archaeopteryx*? Its outer primaries are clearly asymmetric, and the outer vanes, which would form the leading edge in flight, are reduced. Indeed, the very first specimen, the single feather discovered in 1861, is asymmetric: evidence that *Archaeopteryx* could fly was present from the very beginning.[*]

Regardless of the degree to which *Archaeopteryx'* skeleton was reptilian, there can be no doubt that its feathers were indistinguishable in any important ways from those of living birds. Its wings had the basic pattern and proportions of the modern bird's wing; indeed, there has been no essential change in this aerodynamic structure for about 140 million years. So, by the late Jurassic there existed a reptile-bird that had developed the pennaceous feather characteristic of modern birds and that was, as D. B. O. Savile observes, "appreciably advanced aerodynamically" (1957, p. 222).

Establishing that the feathers of *Archaeopteryx* permitted it to fly does little to resolve the question of how feathers came about in the first place. Feathers are unique to birds, and no known structure intermediate between scales and feathers has been identified. Nevertheless,

---

[*] A historical digression: The presence of feather impressions on the leg of the Berlin specimen led William Beebe to propose that a four-wing "tetrapteryx" stage had preceded *Archaeopteryx* in the evolution of flapping flight (1915). Beebe's hypothetical tetrapteryx bird possessed not only feathers extending backward from the wings, but also "hind limb wings" that served as passive parachutes. In reality, the impressions of feathers on the hind limb of the Berlin specimen of *Archaeopteryx* are simply typical contour feathers, similar to those of modern birds.

it is universally accepted by biologists that feathers are directly derived from reptilian scales, with ample evidence provided by Paul Maderson (1972) and Philip Regal (1975).

We know that feathers in modern birds have two physiological functions: thermoregulation and flight. Presumably the very first feathers served one or the other purpose, but not both, because initially feathers would have evolved under selection pressure for only one function. There is no fossil evidence to support either theory, yet, by the same token, neither is precluded. A third alternative to flight and insulation has been suggested from time to time, most recently by Ernst Mayr in 1960, that feathers evolved as a device for communication between the sexes. To be sure, feathers are important in avian courtship displays and thus in choosing mates. But the evolution of almost any structure can be explained as due to sexual selection, and I agree with Philip Regal that "sexual selection as a general evolutionary force, used to explain miscellaneous conditions that are difficult to account for, is unsatisfying" (1975, p. 43). Nor does this explanation account for the distinctive structure of feathers.

The hypothesis that feathers originated as insulating cover takes one of two forms: that they kept heat in or that they kept it out. Currently, the more familiar and popular theory is that they helped to keep the animal warm. Among the living vertebrates, only birds and mammals are "warm-blooded," or endothermic; that is, they maintain high and constant metabolic rates and body temperatures by relying mainly on heat generated from within. In contrast, the reptiles, fishes, and amphibians are "cold-blooded," or ectothermic—their main source of body heat is the ambient environment and their body temperature fluctuates accordingly. It has usually been assumed that endothermy originated twice, once each in mammals and birds, but a currently popular theory holds that dinosaurs were the first endotherms and achieved metabolic rates comparable to those of birds and mammals. If dinosaurs were indeed endothermic, feathers might have been an effective insulating mechanism for them and, once present, could have been a preadaptation for flight.

The foremost proponent of the theory that dinosaurs were warm-blooded and that some had feathers used for thermoregulation is Robert Bakker of Johns Hopkins University. His views can be summarized as follows (1975): (1) dinosaurs achieved erect posture, which is found only among birds and mammals in the living vertebrates; (2) the microscopic structure of certain dinosaur bones is like that of living mammals and can be interpreted to reflect warm-bloodedness; (3) the ratio of predators to prey in fossil deposits of dinosaurs is similar to the ratio found in living communities of mammals and, in Bakker's view, reflects the high metabolic requirement of endothermic predators. All of these arguments are seriously flawed, and the case has not been proven (Benton, 1979).

In the first place, there is certainly no causal relationship between erect posture and endothermy; erect posture was necessary to support the tremendous weight of dinosaurs. And the same microscopic bone structures that Bakker uses as an indication of endothermy are now known to be present in some ectothermic vertebrates and absent in some endotherms (Bouvier, 1977), and they also tend to be associated with large size; thus their presence in dinosaur bones proves nothing. Perhaps the most flawed of Bakker's arguments is the one concerning the predator-prey ratio of dinosaurs (Tracy, 1976). To begin with, statistics based on fossil deposits are notoriously unreliable, because such deposits do not accurately reflect either the number of species in the fauna or the number of animals in each species. Even more important, Bakker's calculations are based on the unwarranted assumption that large carnivorous dinosaurs were primary predators, that is, fed only on herbivorous dinosaurs. There is no reason to believe that the carnivores did not feed on a great diversity of dinosaurs, including the young of all species (which are noticeably absent from the fossil record), or that they did not also feed on carrion. Besides, many adult herbivores, which Bakker thought constituted a large part of the carnivores' diet, were so large that, like adult elephants today, they were probably almost immune to predation. Finally, no feathered dinosaur that would support Bakker's theory has ever been discovered. In many specimens of dinosaurs, the skin has been preserved, and in each case it is typically reptilian.

In fact, it is very likely that dinosaurs were not endothermic. Probably they had a wide range of activity levels, and in most cases their size alone would have resulted in a relatively constant and high body temperature during the warm climates that prevailed in their lifetime. In the tropical and subtropical Jurassic and Cretaceous Periods, there was probably little daily or seasonal temperature change, and under those conditions we would expect ectotherms, not endotherms, to evolve the large size seen in most dinosaurs. Moreover, most dinosaurs had small brains and exhibited indeterminate growth, two characteristics of ectothermic vertebrates (Feduccia 1973). Supporting the idea that dinosaurs were ectothermic is evidence presented by Paul A. Johnston (1979) that dinosaur teeth had growth rings. Such growth rings are produced by variation in the growth rate of living ectotherms, and their presence in dinosaur specimens suggests that in those animals also the growth rate fluctuated with the seasons.

In 1975 Philip Regal proposed another thermoregulatory theory, that feathers may have evolved from reptilian scales to serve as shields against hot sunlight. Regal has shown that scales in several genera of modern lizards are relatively more elongated in warm climates than in cooler ones, and he argues from his experiments that the longer scales act as a barrier against solar radiation. He infers that elongated scales,

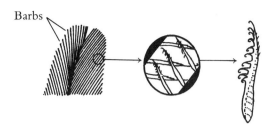

Barbs

The end of a typical contour feather magnified to show: (center) the arrangement of the tiny barbules with their minute hooklets to form an interlocking mechanism between the adjacent barbs and (right) a highly magnified barbule. (After Rawles, 1960.)

then feathers, would have served first as a barrier to influx of heat; then, after endothermy had evolved as a necessary adaptation to maintain flight, the feathers would have prevented heat loss. But this hypothesis is not convincing because it does not satisfactorily account for the complex microarchitecture of the avian feather.

Indeed, the simplest and most profound objection to all thermoregulatory theories is: why feathers? Feathers are extremely complex both structurally and embryologically. They have great resilience, a graded flexibility, and an unusually high strength-to-weight ratio. When a feather is struck a blow, the structure will momentarily split apart, but microscopic hooklets on the tiny barbules connecting the barbs will quickly reattach themselves and reestablish the feather's smooth aerodynamic contour. Moreover, the arrangement of feathers permits the development of slotted wings, which produce high lift at low speed and allow for streamlined airflow (Savile, 1962). For purposes of thermoregulation, why not a simpler structure, such as mammalian hair? In the flightless ratites—the ostrich, rhea, cassowary, and kiwi—for which feathers have only thermoregulatory value, they are very loosely constructed and superficially resemble hair. Indeed, the fluffy, hairlike feathers of many flightless species, such as the rail *Atlantisia rogersi,* give them a mouselike appearance. This difference in feather structure is more than superficial; scanning electron micrographs show that the feathers of flightless forms have lost the hooklets and barbules typical of flight feathers. In short, the release from strong selection pressure to maintain aerodynamic feathers results in a loss of their distinctive characteristics.

The theory that feathers evolved directly for flight was promoted by Heilmann (1926) and has recently been reviewed by Kenneth C. Parkes (1966), Curator of Birds at the Carnegie Museum of Natural History in Pittsburgh. This model pictures the predecessors of birds as highly active, arboreal creatures that took to jumping from branch to branch, as many modern animals do. Savile has shown that the slightest fringe of elongated scale or proto-feather along the trailing edge of the forelimb would have an immediate advantage in parachuting or jumping; at this stage balance would be required, but little or no ability to steer. As he points out, such elongation "is clearly adaptive in protecting from injury in accidental falls, as an escape mechanism and in pursuit of prey" (1962, p. 161). If any elongation of these scales was

The small flightless rail *Atlantisia rogersi,* from Inaccessible Island; its feathers are decomposed and superficially hairlike. (Drawing by Sigrid K. James, after Lowe, 1928a.)

Scanning electron micrographs of feather barbules, offering evidence that feathers originated for flight. With the evolution of flightlessness the feathers become simpler and simpler, losing the complex hooklets and eventually becoming hairlike. At the upper left are the ends of the barbules of a breast feather of a tinamou, a flying bird, magnified 400 times; note the tiny hooklets that join the barbules to give the feather its smooth, aerodynamic contour. At the upper right are the ends of the barbules from a breast feather of a kiwi, a completely flightless bird, magnified 400 times; only the vestiges of the hooklets remain. At the lower left is a barb of the kiwi feather, magnified 80 times, note the fuzzy, hairlike appearance. At the lower right is a barb of a cassowary, magnified 80 times; note the complete absence of hooklets and the very hairlike appearance. (Photos by the author, Mary-Jacque Mann, and Susann G. Braden; courtesy of the Smithsonian SEM Laboratory.)

immediately adaptive, then the emergence of feathers as an aid to air-borne travel can be explained without recourse to preadaptations of one sort or another. The problem of accounting for the adaptiveness of stages intermediate between scales and feathers disappears.

Consider an analogy: if a common gray or red squirrel accidentally falls from a branch, or is shaken from it, the fall at first appears almost vertical. But instead of falling to the ground willy-nilly, the animal spreads its limbs and assumes the attitude typical of the flying (more accurately, gliding) squirrels. This maneuver allows the squirrel to swerve at an angle of as much as 60° and land relatively lightly. Thus, in arboreal animals, jumping and parachuting are immediately adaptive, and it is a short step to the evolution of a true patagium to permit gliding.

To do more than glide, *Archaeopteryx* needed not only its aerodynamic feathers but a skeletal architecture that would allow its muscles to produce the powerful flapping required to maintain it in the air. Many scientists, notably Gavin de Beer, former director of the British Museum (Natural History), have pointed out that the coracoid and other structures of the pectoral girdle in *Archaeopteryx* are weakly developed compared with those of modern flying birds, and that the sternum is not preserved in any of the fossil specimens. The absence of a fossilized sternum, to which the powerful flight muscles would have been attached, does not mean that it was not present in the living creature. It could well have been cartilaginous, inasmuch as the structure was an innovation in birds, and cartilage would not have been preserved in the fossil. "That birds with largely cartilaginous sterna," as Parkes has pointed out, "are capable of adequate flapping flight is well illustrated by the precociously flying chicks of modern gallinaceous birds. I regard the sternal structure of *Archaeopteryx*, therefore, as an open question and would not use it as either evidence for or against the ability to fly" (1976, p. 79). And Storrs Olson of the Smithsonian Institution has shown that "at least in rails, even after ossification of the sternum has begun, the cartilaginous outline of the carina has still not reached its fullest development. In its early stages, the developing sternum of flying rails goes through stages resembling the ossified sternum of various flightless forms" (1973, p. 35).

The one feature of *Archaeopteryx*, other than feathers, that is unique to birds is the furcula. The London specimen has a furcula that would be considered very large in a modern bird, even hypertrophied relative to the furculas of modern birds of the same size. Some workers, such as Gavin de Beer and John Ostrom, have paid scant attention to this important structure, Ostrom merely asking, "Did it function as a transverse spacer between the shoulder sockets?" (1976, p. 11). But Ostrom also concedes that it is the one feature of *Archaeopteryx'* skeleton that is strictly avian. Storrs Olson and I (1979) have argued that the best interpretation of this robust furcula is that it served as the

Left side of the pectoral girdle of the American golden-eye (*Bucephala clangula*), showing the furcula and the extensive coraco-clavicular membrane, where the pectoralis muscle has its main origin. (From Olson and Feduccia, 1979, courtesy of *Nature*; drawing by Jaquin Schulz, after Sy, 1936.)

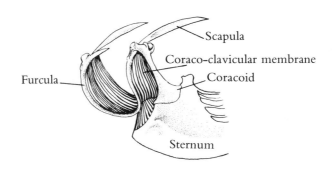

Right side of the pectoral girdle of the pigeon (*Columba livia*), showing the action of the supracoracoideus muscle and the extensive area of the sternum it occupies. The pectoralis muscle attaches to the sternum only on those areas that are stippled. (From Olson and Feduccia, 1979, courtesy of *Nature*; drawing by Jaquin Schulz, after George and Berger, 1966.)

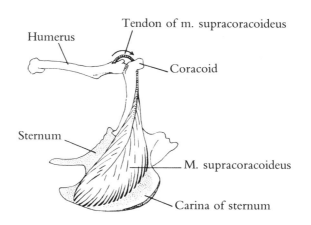

principal site of origin of a well-developed pectoralis muscle, which would have been responsible for the power stroke of the wing. It is a widespread misconception of the pectoral girdle in birds to assume that the keel of the sternum is the main site for attachment of the massive pectoralis. In reality, this muscle originates to a much greater extent from the furcula and the coraco-clavicular membrane, which extends from the furcula to the coracoid. The posterior fibers of the pectoralis originate on the sternum only where the supracoracoideus, the muscle largely responsible for effecting the wing's recovery stroke in modern birds, is *not* present—typically only the periphery of the keel and the lateral and posterior margins. The main function of the keel, therefore, is to serve as the site of origin of the supracoracoideus, and the tendon it sends to the humerus through the triosseal canal formed by the junction of the coracoid, scapula, and furcula.

It has often been thought that avian flight would be impossible without a well-developed supracoracoideus muscle with its circuitous tendon. But, as we saw in Chapter 1, this is not true. The dorsal elevators, principally the deltoideus major, can effect the recovery stroke by themselves, as they did in *Archaeopteryx*. Maxheinz J. Sy, a German anatomist, proved this when he cut the tendons of the supracoracoideus in living crows and pigeons (1936). He found that the birds were capable of normal, sustained flight; the only capacity they lost was the ability to take off from level ground.

Another skeletal feature of *Archaeopteryx* that allies it with the flying birds is the angle of the scapula with the coracoid. In both, the angle is acute; as a result, the distance through which the dorsal elevators must act is shortened and they are thus more powerful. By contrast, the living flightless birds have lost the acute angle; in them the scapula is more nearly perpendicular to the coracoid, and their clavicles are reduced or lost.

In *Archaeopteryx,* then, we see an early stage in the evolution of powered flight. The pectoral muscles accomplish the power stroke, but, in the absence of the supracoracoideus muscle, the dorsal elevators still effect the recovery stroke. Modern birds have an ossified sternum and carina, as well as the supracoracoideus with its tendon attached to the humerus, but this is a single functional complex that is not necessary for flight. No doubt it was superimposed in later birds on a pectoral architecture that was already capable of full flight.

The black coucal (*Centropus grillii*), a 13-inch-long cuckoo of central Africa that is very similar in size and proportions to a small *Archaeopteryx*. *Archaeopteryx* may well have resembled cuckoos in its general appearance. (Drawing by Sigrid K. James, after Austin, 1961.)

Toothed Birds and Divers

During the Cretaceous Period, 135 million to 65 million years ago, the continents as we know them had not yet drifted into their present positions, and many of the land masses of the modern world were covered with vast seaways. One of these divided North America, extending at its maximum expanse from the Gulf of Mexico to the Arctic Circle, spreading out a thousand miles in width from eastern Idaho and Utah across to Iowa. The land itself, still tropical or subtropical in climate, was presided over by dinosaurs such as *Triceratops* and *Tyrannosaurus.* Land birds, having conquered the air with powered flight, were surely gaining cosmopolitan distribution. Feather impressions have been found in Australia in the lower Cretaceous Koowana claystones that date back 135 million years (Talent, Duncan, and Handley 1966; Waldman, 1970). A single feather impression dating from the late Jurassic, coeval with *Archaeopteryx,* was found in a limestone quarry near Lerida, Spain (Condal, 1955). Most of the fossil record of the Cretaceous, however, is from the ancient continental seas, and our knowledge of Cretaceous birds is confined largely to the toothed, principally flightless forms that inhabited the marine environment. As in the case of *Archaeopteryx,* the medium of fossil preservation was limestone, chalky white limestone best exemplified by the White Cliffs of Dover, laid down in the Cretaceous oceans. It is this stone that gives the period its name, from the Latin *creta,* meaning chalk.

Many fossils of the nonavian denizens of these oceans have also been recovered, and they alone could have inspired all subsequent images of "sea monsters." We can imagine huge marine turtles basking near the surface while large pterosaurs such as *Pteranodon* glided overhead with wing spans of up to 22 feet. Even more bizarre were the plesiosaurs, long-necked creatures with fat bodies and wide, paddlelike limbs, often described as extremely large turtles with a snake strung through them. Species of the late Cretaceous ranged from 20 to 40 feet or more in length, and one short-necked Australian form, *Kronosaurus,* had a skull 12 feet long. Large marine lizards called mosasaurs, closely related to the modern monitor lizards, attained lengths of between 15 and 25 feet. There were also myriads of fish, representing the evolutionary mainsprings of our modern bony fishes. The largest of these,

4

Restoration of the late Cretaceous continental seaways that covered much of North America. Toothed birds abounded in these waterways, inhabited also by the giant fish-eating mosasaur *Tylosaurus,* bottom center, a creature that grew to 30 feet in length. The sea turtle *Protostega* had a shell as much as 6 feet long, and in the air the flying reptile *Pteranodon* soared on wings that spanned up to 22 feet. Bony fishes were abundant, no doubt preyed upon by the fishlike reptiles, or ichthyosaurs, represented by *Stenopterygius,* upper right, which provide a remarkable example of convergent evolution with the mammalian porpoises. Another group of reptiles living in the seaways was the plesiosaurs, represented by *Plesiosaurus,* upper left; ranging from 20 to 40 feet in length, these long-necked fish-eaters propelled themselves with strong broad flippers. (Murals by Charles R. Knight; courtesy of the Field Museum of Natural History, Chicago.)

known as *Xiphactinus,* was over 15 feet in length. Also abundant were the fishlike reptiles, or ichthyosaurs, which superficially, at least, resembled modern porpoises.

Cretaceous birds known to have shared this habitat constitute two principal orders: the loonlike Hesperornithiformes and the ternlike Ichthyornithiformes. The oldest known specimen of either order is the hesperornithiform *Enaliornis* from the early Cretaceous of England, almost coeval with *Archaeopteryx* and predating the next well-preserved avian fossils by as much as 50 million years.

Enaliornis is known only from poorly preserved material, but there is no doubt that it, like all hesperornithiforms, was a foot-propelled diver. Thus we can see that birds entered the adaptive zone of diving at about the same time, late Jurassic or early Cretaceous, that they were developing powered flight. Another toothed bird of the Cretaceous is the stout, ternlike ichthyornithiform *Ichthyornis* ("fish bird"), a small-footed form with large wings. While undoubtedly a sideline of avian evolution (its link with the terns is merely a descriptive convenience), *Ichthyornis* is the oldest known bird having a keeled sternum similar to that of modern birds. Both the hesperornithiforms and the ichthyornithiforms died out at the same time the dinosaurs disappeared, at the close of the Cretaceous Period, the hesperornithiforms after having attained a high degree of adaptation for diving.

The hesperornithiform birds are very distinctive from all other known birds and have been placed in their own subclass, the Odontognathae (*odon,* tooth + *gnathos,* jaw), while the ichthyornithiform birds may possibly be allied with the shorebirds. Both groups exhibit a feature reminiscent of *Archaeopteryx* that has generated controversy from the time of these birds' discovery until the present: the reptilian carry-over of teeth.

In considering the Cretaceous toothed birds it is helpful to keep in mind that their discovery followed by only a few years the discovery of *Archaeopteryx,* and occurred while vestiges of reptilian ancestry in birds were still confounding much of the scientific world. It was while the disputes between the likes of Huxley and Owen were still echoing through the museums of Europe that other men of science were making their way across the North American badlands in search of new fossils, many of which were lying exposed on the surface ready for the taking. The richest vein for this "bone rush" was the upper Cretaceous chalk sediments that constitute the Niobrara Formation, most fully exposed in Nebraska and central and western Kansas.

Not surprisingly, the first discovery of a Cretaceous toothed bird from the Cretaceous seaways, that of *Hesperornis* ("western bird"), was made by O. C. Marsh. His own account, taken from his now classic monograph *Odontornithes* (1880), gives some flavor of the times and of the conditions under which this work was carried out:

Yale University expedition of 1870 in the field near Bridger, Wyoming. O. C. Marsh is standing in the center holding a rifle. This was among the first of the "student" expeditions, and George Bird Grinnell of the class of 1870 (third from left) later wrote that probably none of the lot, except the leader, "had any motive for going other than the hope of adventure with wild animals or wild Indians." Reclining on the left is Eli Whitney (class of 1869), grandson of the inventor of the cotton gin. (Courtesy of John H. Ostrom and the Peabody Museum of Natural History, Yale University.)

Recent photographs of the upper Cretaceous chalk deposits of the Niobrara Formation in western Kansas (far right). *Hesperornis* is known from this region, where it flourished along with mosasaurs, plesiosaurs, and a great variety of fish and other marine life. The photo at near right shows the tools of the paleontologist alongside the fin of a large Cretaceous fish. (Photos by the author.)

The first Bird fossil discovered in this region was the lower end of the tibia of *Hesperornis* [the foot-propelled diver from which the order Hesperornithiformes takes its name], found by the writer in December, 1870, near the Smoky Hill River in Western Kansas. Specimens belonging to another genus . . . were discovered on the same expedition. The extreme cold, and danger from hostile Indians, rendered a careful exploration at that time impossible.

In June of the following year, the writer again visited the same region, with a larger party, and a stronger escort of United States troops, and was rewarded by the discovery of the skeleton which forms the type of *Hesperornis regalis,* Marsh. Various other remains . . . were secured, and have since been described by the writer. Although the fossils obtained during two months of exploration were important, the results of this trip did not equal our expectations, owing in part to the extreme heat (110° to 120° Fahrenheit, in the shade) which, causing sunstroke and fever, weakened and discouraged guides and explorers alike.   (1880, p. 2)

These first specimens of *Hesperornis* showed that it had very large feet, diminutive wings, and a flat, unkeeled sternum, indicating it could not fly. But the fossils were headless, and thus the prospect of debate over teeth in birds was postponed. Then in 1872 Marsh's colleague Benjamin F. Mudge recovered from the Niobrara chalk the fossil of what was obviously a small bird with strong wing bones indicative of powered flight. This was the ternlike *Ichthyornis,* which was, unfortunately, also thought to be headless. However, a portion of the lower jaw was retained in the slab. Mudge sent the specimen to Marsh, who gave it the name *Ichthyornis dispar* and identified the jaw on the slab as coming from a new species of small reptile that he called *Colonosaurus mudgei.* However, it was not long before Marsh was forced to change his mind: "When the remains of this species were first described, the portion of the lower jaws found with them were regarded by the writer as reptilian; the possibility of their forming part of the same skeleton, although considered at the time, was deemed insufficiently strong to be placed on record. On subsequently removing the surrounding shale, the skull and additional portion of both jaws were brought to light, so that there can not now be a reasonable doubt that all are part of the same bird" (1873, p. 162).

Front view of the sternum of *Hesperornis,* showing that it is flat and unkeeled. The lack of a carina indicates that the bird had no flight muscles and therefore could not fly. The clavicles are not fused to form the furcula typical of most modern birds, and the wing, so far as is known, consisted only of a vestigial humerus. (After Heilmann, 1926.)

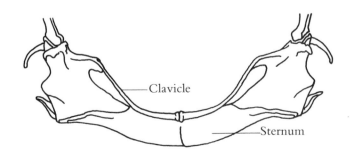

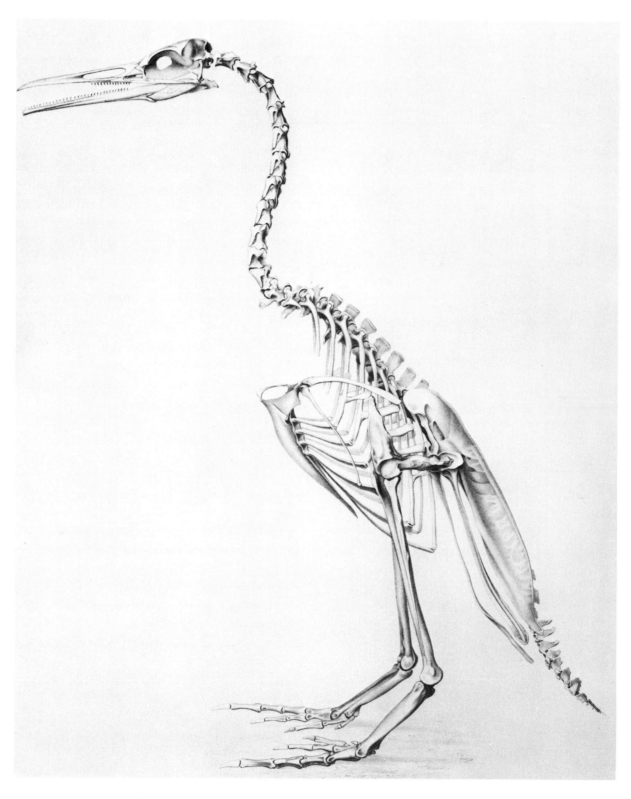

Skeleton of *Hesperornis* from Marsh's
classic monograph *Odontornithes* (1880).
Marsh envisioned the bird as a large
flightless form superficially similar to
modern loons.

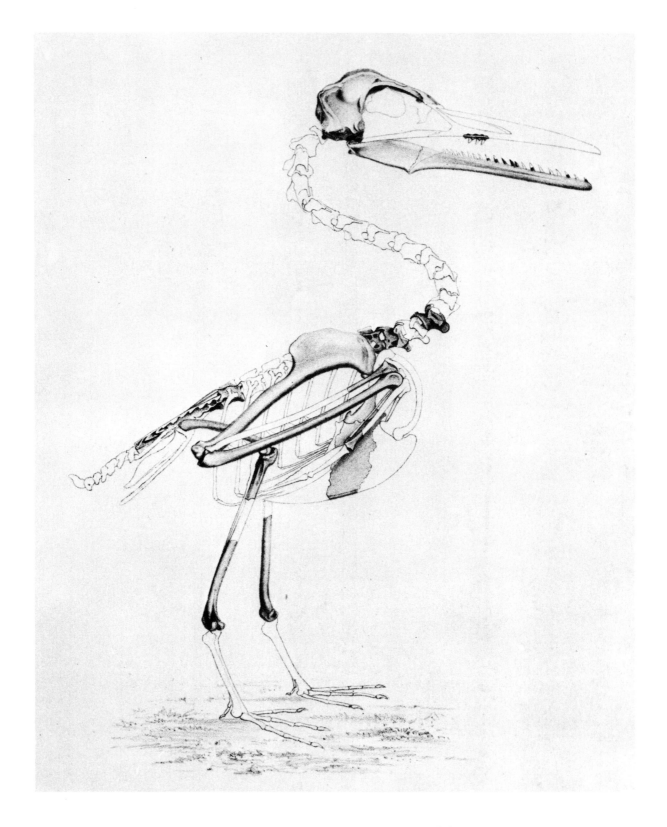

Skeleton of *Ichthyornis* from Marsh's
classic monograph *Odontornithes* (1880).
Note the large wing bones and keeled
sternum.

Artist's reconstruction of the ternlike Cretaceous toothed bird *Ichthyornis*. Pierce Brodkorb has described the skeleton of *Ichthyornis* as having considerable similarity to the skeletons of the rhinoceros auklet (*Cerorhinca monocerata*) and the tufted puffin (*Lunda cirrhata*) (Brodkorb, 1971). (Drawing by Sigrid K. James.)

It was two years later that Marsh published his description of the teeth in *Hesperornis regalis,* the foot-propelled diver. This was 1875, the year of the discovery of the Berlin specimen of *Archaeopteryx.* Nonetheless, the controversy over ancient toothed birds was not completely laid to rest. As recently as the 1950s Joseph Gregory restudied Marsh's types and concluded that the jaw found with *Ichthyornis* was actually that of a small or juvenile marine lizard (Gregory, 1951, 1952). He even went so far as to identify the jaw as coming from a specific genus of mosasaur, *Clidastes.* But no small mosasaur approaching the size of *Ichthyornis* has ever been found, and though Gregory's arguments were accepted by some for a time, it is now certain that *Ichthyornis* did have teeth.

Over the years Marsh described six species of *Ichthyornis* from the Smoky Hill Chalk of the Niobrara Formation, and a seventh species from the upper Cretaceous Austin Chalk of Texas. Recently, Storrs Olson (1975a) has shown that a fossil from the upper Cretaceous Selma Chalk of Alabama that was originally described as the small ibis *Plegadornis* is really *Ichthyornis,* a finding that indicates a widespread occurrence of *Ichthyornis* over North America. Marsh also named a species very similar to *Ichthyornis, Apatornis celer,* placing it in its own family, the Apatornithidae. Currently there are two known species of *Apatornis,* but the fossil remains are too fragmentary to allow reliable reconstruction of the bird. What we can say about the habits of *Ichthyornis* and *Apatornis* in life is therefore limited to what we can infer from their structure and from the location in which remains were found. It does seem abundantly clear that with strong powers of flight, long jaws and recurved teeth for capturing prey, these birds were well adapted for the life of volant carnivores in the Cretaceous seaways.

The hesperornithiform birds were quite differently adapted and show evidence of a great diversity and worldwide distribution during the Cretaceous. Larry D. Martin of the University of Kansas, who has been studying the hesperornithiforms for several years, thinks that as many as 7 genera and 13 species may have existed. In addition to *Hesperornis,* the distinctive genus *Baptornis* is now known from rather extensive material, described in great detail by Martin and James Tate (1976). Another genus, *Coniornis,* is known from the late Cretaceous of Montana. *Coniornis* and *Hesperornis* are included in the family Hesperornithidae; *Baptornis* and *Neogaeornis,* from the late Cretaceous of Kansas and Chile, respectively, are placed in the Baptornithidae.

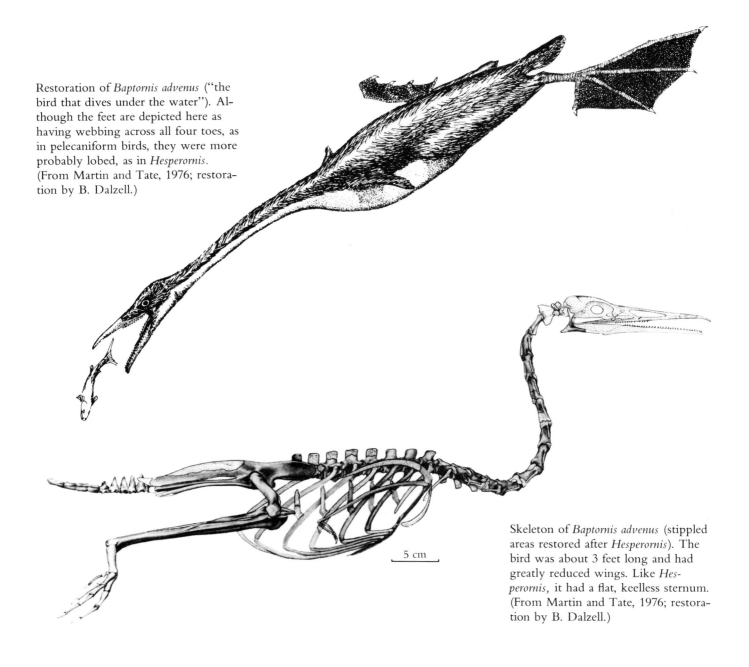

Restoration of *Baptornis advenus* ("the bird that dives under the water"). Although the feet are depicted here as having webbing across all four toes, as in pelecaniform birds, they were more probably lobed, as in *Hesperornis.* (From Martin and Tate, 1976; restoration by B. Dalzell.)

5 cm

Skeleton of *Baptornis advenus* (stippled areas restored after *Hesperornis*). The bird was about 3 feet long and had greatly reduced wings. Like *Hesperornis,* it had a flat, keelless sternum. (From Martin and Tate, 1976; restoration by B. Dalzell.)

Restoration of *Hesperornis regalis,* the
largest bird in the genus, about 5 feet
long. (From Lucas, 1901.)

One specimen of *Hesperornis* has recently been reported from an estuarine deposit in Alberta, Canada (Fox, 1974), and Larry Martin is currently describing a freshwater subfamily of hesperornithiform birds from the late Cretaceous of South Dakota. But the marine environment is by far the more commonly associated habitat. Martin has suggested that the hesperornithiforms nested in rookeries on isolated coastlines or perhaps on islands in the Cretaceous seaways. The upper Cretaceous Niobrara Chalk in Kansas and elsewhere is a carbonate deposit that shows no evidence of any continental deposits, and the apparent absence of a nearby shoreline would imply that the hesperornithiforms, as well as the pteranodons and ichthyornithiforms whose fossils were found in these same deposits, were accustomed to venturing many hundreds of miles into the open sea (Martin and Tate, 1976). Dale A. Russell (1967) has reported remains of subadults of *Hesperornis* from the region of the Anderson River in Canada at a latitude of 69° north, and has suggested that a nesting colony may have existed nearby. Could it be that *Hesperornis* migrated to northern breeding grounds near the Arctic rim of the continent? It is also possible, as indicated by the distances the birds ventured into the open sea, that *Hesperornis,* like the ichthyosaurs, gave birth to live young and never ventured onto dry land. We know that all hesperornithiforms would have been clumsy on land, because they could not fly and could only propel themselves with their large hind feet. It is possible that their habits were in some ways like those of modern diving mammals such as seals.

Heilmann's life reconstruction of *Hesperornis regalis*. (From Heilmann, 1926.)

For the hesperornithiforms, selection favored adaptations more like those of the Mesozoic marine mammals and marine reptiles than like those associated with modern birds. In contrast to the adaptations for light weight favored in volant birds, including even the toothed *Ichthyornis,* adaptations for foot-propelled diving strive to overcome light weight and its resultant buoyancy. The hesperornithiforms, like the marine mammals and reptiles of their era, had dense, heavy, non-pneumatic bones. Martin has suggested that these dense bones enabled them to swim slightly beneath the surface, as do the modern snake-birds.

In most other skeletal features, however, the hesperornithiforms paralleled the modern grebes and loons, although there is no phylogenetic relationship between the Cretaceous hesperornithiforms and the modern foot-propelled divers. At least one species of *Hesperornis* is similar in size to modern grebes, though *Hesperornis regalis* is almost 5 feet long. As in all divers, the foot bones of the hesperornithiforms were laterally compressed, allowing a streamlined forward sweep through the water. These ancient birds also share with grebes the special adaptations of the toes of the hind foot that allow them to rotate sideways on the recovery stroke. It is probable that, also as in grebes, the toes were lobed, with each toe separately fringed with webbing, instead of fully webbed. Other shared adaptations include a reduced air-sac volume, a leg that is united with the body musculature nearly to the ankle joint, a long and narrow pelvis, a short femur, and a long tibiotarsus with a long bony extension to which the powerful extensor muscles of the leg are attached. This extension, among other things, demonstrates that the hesperornithiforms are merely convergent with, rather than related to, the loons and grebes. In *Hesperornis* it is formed only by the kneecap, or patella. In loons it is an exclusive extension of the tibiotarsus called the cnemial crest; in grebes it is compounded from both the cnemial crest and the patella.

Highly specialized foot-propelled divers actually arose several different times quite independently. The hesperornithiforms, as we have seen, were an evolutionary dead end, having died out at the end of the Cretaceous Period. In the mid-Tertiary there evolved another group, the cormorants and snakebirds, both modified derivatives of pelecaniform stock. Many of the Anseriformes (ducks, geese, swans) have also evolved diving adaptations of various sorts. The recently extinct California goose *Chendytes* was a totally flightless foot-propelled diver, and several lines of the duck assemblage are so highly adapted for foot-propelled diving that they very seldom venture onto land. The North American ruddy duck (*Oxyura jamaicensis*), for example, "cannot

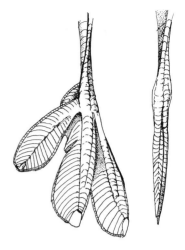

The paddlelike, lobate toes of grebes: (left) in position for the backward power stroke; (right) in position for the recovery stroke, in which the toes fold sideways by rotation to minimize friction. Hesperornithiform birds employed a similar method of toe rotation, as is indicated by the bony structures of their toes, and therefore apparently had lobate webbing. (Adapted from Peterson, 1963.)

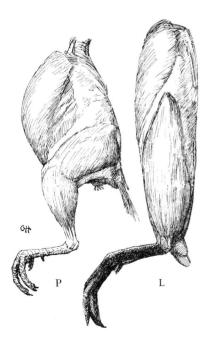

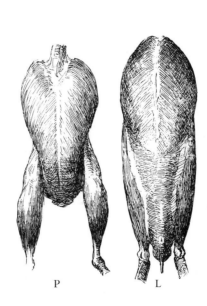

Comparison of skinned bodies of a pheasant (*P*) and a loon (*L*) in lateral (left) and ventral (right) views, illustrating how the loon's leg musculature has, as a diving adaptation, become incorporated into the body mass. (From Heilmann, 1926.)

The pied-billed grebe (*Podilymbus podiceps*). (Drawing by Yvonne Lee.)

The common loon (*Gavia immer*). (Drawing by Yvonne Lee.)

walk on land for more than a few steps without falling on its breast" (Raikow, 1970, p. 5). But the champion among the many diving ducks is the old-squaw (*Clangula hyemalis*), which has been recorded at depths of about 180 feet, the same as for the common loon (*Gavia immer*). Finally, the loons and grebes, although formerly classified together, undoubtedly represent independently evolved lines of foot-propelled divers. Grebes (order Podicipediformes) are probably derived from gruiform stock, while loons are suggested by Robert W. Storer (1960) of the University of Michigan to have derived from ancient shorebird (charadriiform) stock. In the fossil record grebes are known as far back as the early Miocene, about 25 million years ago, but the similarity between ancient and modern species prevents our gaining much insight into evolutionary relationships.

We know of 19 living species of grebes, distributed worldwide in freshwater lakes and ponds, some of which migrate great distances to winter near coastal waters. The lobate webbing of their feet is known only in the phylogenetically distant phalaropes (order Charadriiformes, family Phalaropodidae), the coots (Gruiformes, Rallidae), the finfoots (Gruiformes, Heliornithidae), and, as we have seen, the extinct hesperornithiforms. Lobate webbing thus represents a remarkable example of convergent evolution. Generally weak flyers, grebes have shown a tendency to become nearly flightless, as in the Atitlan grebe of Guatemala (*Podiceps gigas*); or totally flightless, as in the nearly keelless short-winged grebe (*Centropelma micropterum*) of Lake Titicaca, on the border between Peru and Bolivia.

Modern loons (Gaviiformes), by contrast, have a large keel and are strong flyers. The primitive teal-sized loon *Colymboides minutus* is well represented in upper Oligocene and lower Miocene fossil deposits (Storer, 1956), but it was not as highly adapted for diving as the modern loons. The oldest fossil to be described as a loon is *Lonchodytes* from the late Cretaceous of North America, but it has now been shown to be a shorebird (Olson and Feduccia, 1980a). The oldest reli-

Phylogenetic trees of the toothed divers, loons, shorebirds, gulls, auks, penguins, and petrels. (From Storer, 1960.)

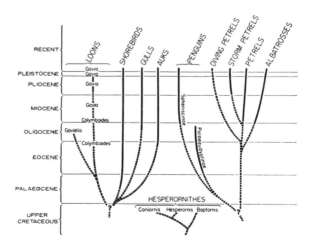

SOUTHERN HEMISPHERE Petrel-Penguin Stock	Adaptive stage	NORTHERN HEMISPHERE Gull-Auk Stock
Penguins	Wings used for submarine flight only STAGE C	Great Auk
Diving Petrels	Wings used for both submarine and aerial flight STAGE B	Razor-Bill
Petrels	Wings used for aerial flight only STAGE A	Gulls

Parallel adaptive stages in the evolution of two stocks of wing-propelled divers, one in the Southern and one in the Northern Hemisphere. (From Storer, 1960.)

able record for loons is the species *Colymboides anglicus,* which goes back to the early Eocene of England. A genus apparently unrelated to modern loons, *Gaviella,* dates back to the Oligocene of Wyoming. But the modern genus *Gavia* first appears in the late Miocene.

Wing-propelled divers have arisen from at least three independent evolutionary lineages, but not until after the close of the Cretaceous, in Cenozoic time. From the petrels (Procellariiformes), diving petrels (Pelecanoididae) evolved in the Southern Hemisphere. The Southern Hemisphere penguins (Sphenisciformes) are also thought to be derived from procellariiform ancestors. In the Northern Hemisphere, wing-propelled divers are known among the auks and allies (Alcidae), both living and extinct, forms derived from shorebird ancestry. Referred to collectively by ornithologists as alcids, these birds include the auks, auklets, murres, murrelets, guillemots, dovekies, and puffins.

Perhaps the birds most highly adapted for wing-propelled diving, which might be described as "flying" under water, are the penguins. Ancient birds whose existence has been documented by abundant fossils dating back to the Eocene, penguins have always been confined to the oceans of the Southern Hemisphere, their northernmost range now represented by one species living in the Galápagos in the cold Humboldt Current. Their most obvious counterparts in the Northern Hemisphere are wing-propelled diving auks.

Penguins are so distinctive from all other living birds that the course of their evolution was debated for years. In 1933 one ornithologist, Percy Lowe, even proposed that penguins were derived not from flying ancestors but from primitive flightless birds that took to the water. But George Gaylord Simpson (1946, 1975, 1976), who has stud-

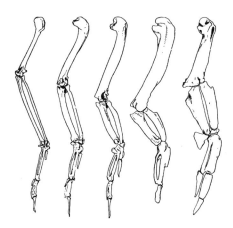

From left to right, wing skeletons of a gull (*Larus*), razor-billed auk (*Alca*), great auk (*Pinguinus*), Lucas auk (*Mancalla*), and penguin (*Spheniscus*), showing adaptive stages similar to those through which the penguin flipper evolved. (From Storer, 1960.)

ied penguins more thoroughly than perhaps any other person, argues convincingly that penguins evolved from flying ancestors, a view now generally accepted. Developing Simpson's ideas further, Robert Storer (1960) argues that ecological equivalents for the various stages of wing-propelled diving evolved in different groups in the Northern and Southern Hemispheres. In the earliest stage, represented by the modern gulls in the north and the true petrels in the south, wings were used only for flight in the air. Then came a compromise stage in which wings were used both for submarine and for aerial flight; this stage is represented today by the Southern Hemisphere diving petrels and the Northern Hemisphere razor-billed auks. Ultimately, the wings came to be used for submarine flight only, a stage represented in the Southern Hemisphere by the penguins, and in the Northern Hemisphere by the now extinct great auks.

Storer (1960) also used five examples from different avian groups to illustrate the probable course of evolution that produced the wings of penguins. The completely aerial stage might be represented by a gull, followed by the compromise adaptation represented by the razor-billed auk. The now extinct great auk would represent a stage shortly after the loss of aerial flight; then would come the Pliocene auklike genus *Mancalla,* which has a still more penguinlike morphology; and finally the penguins themselves.

The association of penguins and auks has a long tradition. The word *penguin* was, in fact, originally used to designate the extinct flightless great auk of the North Atlantic. These birds, which stood over 2 feet tall, bred on some of the islands off Newfoundland, Iceland, and even Britain. Vast hordes were exterminated by sailors, the last auks having been killed in 1844. The species wintered south to New England in the western Atlantic and to Spain in the eastern Atlantic, and fossils found in locations from Florida to Italy indicate a much more extensive distribution in the past. Recently, Storrs Olson (1977a) has described the ancestor of the great auk from lower Pliocene deposits in North Carolina. This fossil species, *Pinguinus alfrednewtoni,* was quite similar in size and proportions to the Recent great auk, *P. impennis,* but its skeleton was slightly less specialized for wing-propelled locomotion. So little evolutionary change between the Recent great auk and its five-million-year-old ancestor is amazing.

Intermediate between the great auks and penguins in structural specialization for wing-propelled diving were the flightless Lucas auks. They were named for Frederick Lucas, who described the first species, *Mancalla californiensis.* Lucas auks are known from upper Miocene to Pleistocene deposits along the coast of California, and a less specialized forerunner is known from the Miocene of Orange County, California. These fossils have been described in detail by the eminent avian paleontologist Hildegarde Howard (1966, 1970), Chief Curator Emeritus of the Natural History Museum of Los Angeles County.

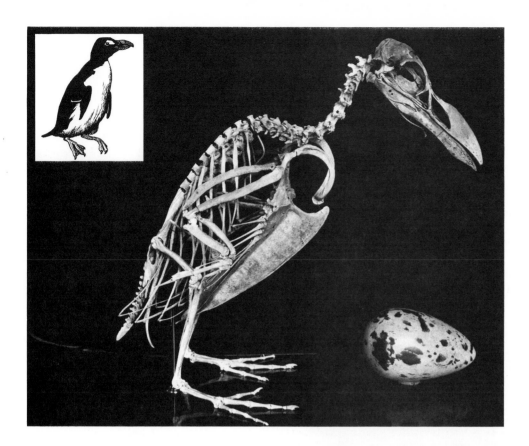

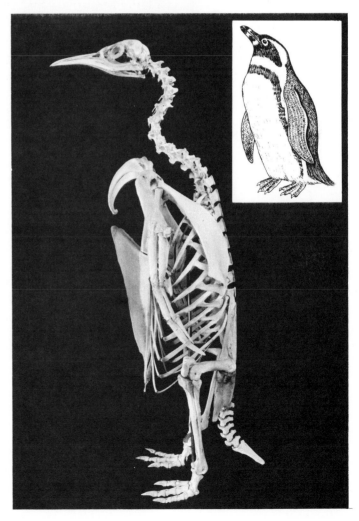

Skeletons of the extinct great auk (above) and a penguin (below), Northern and Southern Hemisphere wing-propelled divers, respectively. The inserts show their appearance in life. (Photos courtesy of the American Museum of Natural History; drawings by Yvonne Lee.)

California's extinct flightless Lucas auk,
Mancalla, and the extinct flightless
goose *Chendytes*: examples of flightless
wing- and foot-propelled divers. (From
Howard, 1947; illustrations by Arminta
Neal; courtesy of D. P. Whistler and
the Natural History Museum of Los
Angeles County.)

Mancalla (left) and *Chendytes* (right)

Mancalla

Chendytes

Reconstruction of the largest species of plotopterid, shown to scale with the outline of the largest living penguin. (From Olson and Hasegawa, *Science,* 206:688–689, November 1979 (cover illustration); drawing by B. Dalzell; copyright 1979 by the American Association for the Advancement of Science.)

Recent discoveries of mid-Tertiary fossils by Storrs Olson and Yoshikazu Hasegawa (1979) indicate that the Northern Hemisphere, specifically the northern Pacific, was inhabited by yet another group of penguinlike birds that converged on the giant penguins of the Southern Hemisphere. This is the fossil family Plotopteridae, the only wing-propelled divers in the order Pelecaniformes (pelicans and allies). This family contains the largest swimming birds known, and one species is estimated to have measured 6 feet from bill to tip of tail. Plotopterid specimens have been found in rocks of late Oligocene and early Miocene age in Japan, Washington, and California, and it appears that their extinction occurred at the same time as that of giant penguins. G. G. Simpson's hypothesis for the extinction of the giant penguins by the

A nondiving pelecaniform, the California Miocene pseudo-toothed bird *Osteodontornis orri,* with bony toothlike projections along the sides of the bill rather than true reptilian teeth. Pseudodontorns, which became extinct at the end of the Pliocene, were among the largest flying birds, well adapted for soaring with wing spans as large as 17 feet. They are known from the Eocene of England, the late Miocene of both coasts of North America, and the Pliocene of New Zealand. The picture above shows the fossil slab as discovered, with reconstructions of the skeleton, musculature, and total form, scaled by a large gull. The life reconstruction at far right shows the bird eating a squid. (Reconstructions by Mark Hallet; courtesy of D. P. Whistler and the Natural History Museum of Los Angeles County.)

Most primitive of the living pelecaniforms, the tropic bird (*Phaethon*), shown in silhouette. (Drawing by Linda M. Hillowe.)

end of the early Miocene is that the niches for pelagic endotherms of that size were occupied by seals and porpoises, both of which were undergoing adaptive radiation at that time. The same would seem to apply to the plotopterids, and thereby to add credence to Simpson's theory.

The order Pelecaniformes itself is not obviously related to any other group of birds, living or extinct, although certain features hint of affinity with the storks and oceanic birds. The earliest trace of the order is the early Eocene remains of a primitive tropic bird called *Prophaethon,* a nondiving form. Modern tropic birds, *Phaethon,* are regarded as primitive within the order, and *Prophaethon* is considered by Colon Harrison and Cyril Walker (1976) to show some affinity with both the Charadriiformes and the Procellariiformes.

A flightless foot-propelled diver, the
Galápagos cormorant (*Phalacrocorax
harrisi*), shown sunning what remains
of its once powerful wings. (Drawing
by Melissa Marshall.)

In addition to the wing-propelled plotopterids, the order Pelecaniformes has produced several lines of foot-propelled divers. The snake-
birds (Anhingidae) are strong divers and swimmers adapted for spear-
ing fish with their sharp beaks. Cormorants (*Phalacrocoracidae*) are also
very powerful foot-propelled divers, and one species, the Galápagos
cormorant (*Phalacrocorax harrisi*) has become completely flightless.
Boobies and gannets (Sulidae) are also strongly adapted and are perhaps the grandest aerial divers of them all, dropping from 30 to 100
feet through the air to descend great depths under the water using their
powerful feet and half-opened wings.

Shorebirds, Ducks, and Waders

5

Time and again during his long voyage on H.M.S. *Beagle* (1831–1835), Charles Darwin was fascinated by the flamingos he encountered in Argentina, Chile, and the Galápagos, wondering how these strange creatures could exist on lakes that for half a year became covered with stark white salt, at times over a foot thick. He did not fully understand that flamingos are tied to saline lakes with large algal blooms, where these master strainers make their livelihood by filtering algae and other small aquatic creatures from the water. Little did Darwin know that in these briny inland lakes he was observing the highly specialized relicts of a strange lineage of evolution originating from ancient filter-feeding, stiltlike shorebirds. Flamingos, today confined to several isolated areas of the earth, once enjoyed worldwide distribution and were represented by two evolutionary lines.

The surviving six species (four of some authors) are all quite similar in anatomy. The largest, the greater flamingo (*Phoenicopterus ruber roseus*), and the smaller lesser flamingo (*Phoeniconaias minor*) occur widely in the Old World, and are especially prevalent in East Africa's Rift Valley. The lesser flamingo is the most numerous species in Africa, while the greater flamingo is more widespread, nesting not only in Kenya, but also from the shores of the Mediterranean east to western India and Ceylon. The other four species are confined to the New World, with one, the American flamingo (*Phoenicopterus ruber ruber*), ranging from the Bahamas through Yucatan and northwestern South America to the Galápagos. The remaining three, the Chilean, Andean, and James' flamingos (respectively, *Phoenicopterus chilensis*, *Phoenicoparrus andinus*, and *Phoenicoparrus jamesi*), live primarily in the soda lakes of the high Andean plateaus.

Lake Nakuru in Kenya is a world-famous haunt of flamingos. Located in the Rift Valley, Nakuru is a shallow, alkaline lake, about 24 square miles in extent, that at times may have concentrations of more than a million flamingos. One such swarm inspired Roger Tory Peterson to label it "the most fabulous bird spectacle in the world." What is it about the seemingly sterile lakes of the Rift Valley that attracts such huge aggregations of birds? Although apparently barren, these lakes actually produce a great abundance of small animal and plant life at

The American flamingo (*Phoenicopterus ruber ruber*). "I met with these birds wherever there were lakes of brine," wrote Darwin in August 1833, after a visit to a large alkaline lake near the mouth of the Rio Negro in Argentina. (Drawing by Yvonne Lee.)

A flock of lesser flamingos (*Phoeniconaias minor*) at East Africa's Lake Nakuru. (Photo by Thomas C. Emmel.)

certain times of the year. As Philip Kahl has estimated, "When a million or more lesser flamingos and thousands of greater flamingos congregate on relatively small bodies of water, such as Kenya's Lake Nakuru, they may consume 200 tons of food a day" (1970, p. 279). Flamingos flock together in such vast numbers because of the unpredictability of the food supply. As water levels in different lakes vary, so do salinity and food levels; the flamingos wander from lake to lake, converging on those that contain an abundance of food.

The most characteristic feature of modern flamingos, one that is unique among birds, is their strange decurved bill, superbly designed for filtering algae and other small plants and animals out of the water. Flamingos feed with their bill inverted, the upper bill below the lower; the lower bill pumps against the upper to sieve water (containing algae and other small plants and animals) and mud through slits on the upper bill and toothlike protuberances on the tongue, the pumping organ. The tongue is so big that it prevents large organisms from entering the mouth. Though algae are a very important food, flamingos may feed on a great variety of organisms depending on the habitat, including diatoms, protozoans, small worms, the larvae of insects, small mollusks and crustaceans, and occasionally very small fish.

The various species may feed quite differently, and where two species occur side by side, the ecological niche may be partitioned very finely for harmonious coexistence. On East Africa's flamingo

East Africa's Lake Hannington. The shoreline is literally teeming with flamingos, and the entire lake is dotted with swimming flamingos that feed even out in the deepest portions. (Photo by the author.)

lakes, where both the greater and lesser flamingos occur, the lesser is primarily an algal filter-feeder, straining algae from the upper 2 or 3 inches of the lake. On calm days lesser flamingos swim out into the center of the large lakes and continue to filter the upper layer of water for its rich algal supply. In contrast, the much less numerous greater flamingos, with coarser toothlike projections on the bill and tongue, feed principally on larger items, such as mollusks and crustaceans, that the lesser flamingo cannot strain. The greater flamingo also stirs up the bottom mud with its feet (a behavior known in a number of modern birds), thus scooping up microorganisms in a souplike suspension that it strains along with algae.

Flamingo nests are unique in the world of birds, and all flamingos build more or less the same type. Made of mud, the nests are, depending on the species, 5 to 18 inches tall, about a foot in diameter at the top, and perhaps 15 to 30 inches across the base. In the concave top the female deposits a single egg, which both sexes incubate. Young flamingos are hatched as downy chicks and are very precocious. Several weeks after hatching they are capable of swimming and leave the nest to herd with other youngsters in a large aggregation called a crèche, tended by several adult "nursemaids." Both parents feed the young by regurgitation for up to seven weeks, unerringly locating their own offspring in the huge crèche.

The relationships of flamingos has been one of the most debated issues in avian evolution. There are at least 15 separate studies, each of which lists the flamingos somewhere near either the ducks, geese, and swans (Anseriformes) or the storks, ibises, and herons (Ciconiiformes), long-legged wading birds adapted for life in shallow waters or marshes. Evolutionary relationship with the ducks and geese has been based primarily on the structure of the bill and feet, the development of the young (young flamingos have a straight bill closely resembling that of ducks, and also a plumage of fluffy down like the ducks), and the similarity of duck and flamingo feather parasites. Adult flamingos also make a loud honking sound very like that of geese. The main reason for believing that the flamingos share kinship with the storks, ibises, and herons has been superficial similarity in appearance. But the question is whether flamingos are most closely related to the herons and storks and merely convergent to the anseriform birds, or whether they were derived from the ducks and geese and only later converged toward the stork and heron body form because of their wading habits. Another possibility, of course, is that flamingos were derived from some third group of birds and are similar to both ducks and herons by convergent evolution.

The fossil record of flamingos has been thought to be ancient, but the further one goes back in time, the more flamingo bones resemble those of shorebirds, a similarity that has led to confusion in the diagnosis of Cretaceous bone fragments. The oldest valid flamingo is from the Eocene, but were it not for associated skeletal elements, it undoubtedly would have been classified as a recurvirostrid shorebird, because of similarities to the avocets and stilts of the family Recurvirostridae. In 1931, the German paleontologist Kálmán Lambrecht described the oldest Cretaceous bird, *Gallornis straeleni,* as a representative of the flamingo line on the basis of a portion of a femur and a scrap of humerus, but it is impossible to determine the affinities of Mesozoic birds on the basis of such fragmentary evidence (Olson and Feduccia, 1980a). In 1933, Lambrecht erected a family of Cretaceous flamingos known as the Scaniornithidae, but the entire Mesozoic fossil record of flamingos has proved to be a myth, and this family simply cannot be diagnosed. As for Tertiary forms, aside from the line leading to modern flamingos, there is only one valid group, represented by very abundant fossils from the early Miocene to the early Pliocene of the Northern Hemisphere. These are the swimming flamingos of the family Palaelodidae.

The fossil record of most groups of vertebrates is replete with "missing links" that tell of interrelationships, but until recently there were no fossils that truly linked any orders of modern birds. Then in 1971, students and field parties under the direction of Paul O. McGrew of the University of Wyoming began to discover huge concentrations of associated skeletons of *Presbyornis,* a strange evolutionary mosaic possessing characteristics of several living orders of birds. This versatile filter-feeding bird, which probably had worldwide distribution, has allowed us to completely reevaluate the relationships of shorebirds, modern ducks, and flamingos. The *Presbyornis* fossils come from lower Eocene deposits in the Green River Formation of southwestern Wyoming and southeastern Utah, and date back roughly 50 million years. They have confirmed that shorebirds are the basic ancestral stock for both flamingolike birds and the anseriforms, and that the ciconiiforms have little, if anything, to do with the flamingos or ducks (Feduccia, 1976, 1977b, 1978). Their resemblance to the flamingos, with their long legs for wading, is strictly superficial and the result of convergent evolution. In fact, even the various groups within the Ciconiiformes are not closely related, and it is certain that herons have little to do with either the storks or the ibises (Olson, 1979).

Life reconstruction of *Presbyornis* by John P. O'Neill. Highly colonial in habit, these birds often formed huge nesting and feeding aggregations.

The original *Presbyornis* quarry explored by Paul McGrew and associates, north of Rock Springs, Wyoming, in Sweetwater County. This view shows the Laney escarpment above Parnell Creek in the background. The quarry itself was once part of a vast saline lake of the Eocene Period. The discovery of logs encrusted with algae indicates that this briny lake produced large algal blooms like those found today in the East African alkaline lakes. (Courtesy of Paul O. McGrew.)

The braincase (center) and nasal region of *Presbyornis*, scaled by a penny. This specimen was recovered in the summer of 1975 from the top of Canyon Creek butte, some 95 miles from McGrew's original *Presbyornis* quarry. The V-shaped bifurcation (shown by the arrow) of the nasal hinge region is characteristic of modern flamingos. The constricted region in front of the hinge accommodated the very large nasal glands for salt excretion; salt glands are found in all of the living flamingos, and in almost all other birds that occur either in saline lakes or on or near salt water. (Photo by the author.)

Disassociated skeletons of *Presbyornis* had been discovered long before McGrew's efforts, and were first described, in 1926, by Alexander Wetmore of the Smithsonian Institution as a new family of shorebirds close to the Recurvirostridae, the family containing avocets and stilts. It is an example of Wetmore's perspicacity that he properly identified the fossils as being of shorebird affinity. Even now, had the recently discovered skeletons not been associated, different elements of *Presbyornis* could be described as a duck, because of the skull and bill; a flamingo, because of features in the region of the frontal and nasal bones; or a shorebird, on the basis of certain bones, such as the humerus.

When I first began to study *Presbyornis* in 1971, I tentatively classified it as a flamingolike wader because the postcranial bones were quite similar to those of flamingos. But I had wondered why Wetmore placed *Presbyornis* near the shorebird family Recurvirostridae, and upon making the proper comparisons I was quick to discern that the postcranial anatomy of flamingos and recurvirostrid shorebirds is very similar, and distinctive from that of all other ciconiiform birds. It was this discovery that led me to conclude that flamingos were related to and derived from ancient shorebird stock.

The grayish-green mudstone of McGrew's original *Presbyornis* quarry had, however, supplied more than postcranial bones. Many bills were unearthed, and, of equal interest, the braincases of a number of individuals were preserved with the nasal and frontal bones intact. Both the bills and the braincases were quite ducklike, but the nasal-frontal bones were arranged in a V-shaped conformation found elsewhere only in modern flamingos, in modified form in flamingo adults, but almost exactly similar in their young. In fact, this region of the skull of *Presbyornis,* in size and morphology, is nearly identical to that of a 30-day-old chick of the American flamingo (*Phoenicopterus ruber ruber*). Thus the initial identification of *Presbyornis* as a flamingolike wader with ducklike features of the skull was unavoidable (Feduccia and McGrew, 1974).

During the summer of 1975, McGrew and I collected at another Eocene locality about 95 miles south of the original quarry, a resistant steamboat-shaped butte near the Colorado–Wyoming border called the Canyon Creek butte. This enormous butte preserves part of the shoreline of an Eocene lake, a shoreline that was apparently teeming with the highly colonial *Presbyornis*. In this locality the bills were much better preserved, and we began to see that *Presbyornis* was even more ducklike than we had previously thought.

Since that time my work on the relationships and evolution of ducks and flamingos has been in collaboration with Storrs Olson (Olson and Feduccia, 1980a, 1980b). In one paper (1980a) we describe another fossil from the Eocene that is extremely similar in anatomy to the Recurvirostridae, and shows just how close the flamingo-stilt af-

Views of the Canyon Creek butte, about 300 feet high, in the southern part of Sweetwater County, Wyoming. This butte preserves part of the shoreline of a very large Eocene lake, perhaps the same lake that covered the original *Presbyornis* quarry, 95 miles to the north. Part of the Green River Formation, the butte, as is clear in the picture below, is composed of a number of materials: mottled mudstone interbedded with varicolored sandstone resistant to erosion, some detrital material derived from the Unita Mountains to the southwest, and a few thin layers of tan algal limestone.

Fossil bones of *Presbyornis* project in vast numbers from a thin layer below the rim of the butte. This layer outcrops at the very top of the picture on the right. The picture on the left shows the author examining the *Presbyornis* zone in one of the few places where it can be reached. (Photo at left courtesy of Paul O. McGrew; photos below and at right by the author.)

The Australian banded stilt (*Clado-rhynchus leucocephalus*), in the family Recurvirostridae. It is the closest living link between shorebirds and flamingos (Olson and Feduccia, 1980a). Like flamingos, these stilts are highly colonial filter-feeding denizens of alkaline lakes. Their downy young, like those of flamingos, soon leave the nest to congregate in crèches. (Drawing by Sigrid K. James.)

finity is; this fossil may, in fact, be close to the actual ancestry of flamingos. It also became apparent to us that the flamingolike features of *Presbyornis* are actually primitive shorebird features, and therefore tell us only that flamingos are ultimately derived from ancient shorebirds. With the discovery in 1977 of a completely articulated skull of *Presbyornis* at Canyon Creek butte, the affinity between *Presbyornis* and ducks became even clearer. Collected by Storrs Olson and Robert J. Emry of the Smithsonian Institution, this skull is so similar in overall architecture to duck skulls, with only a few flamingo characteristics, that there can no longer be any doubt that *Presbyornis* was on the line leading to ducks and not to modern flamingos.

But the flamingolike nasal-frontal region may still link *Presbyornis* and the flamingos, although their divergence was surely an ancient one. The evolutionary choice in the highly colonial filter-feeding ancestors was apparently between a tongue accommodated by the upper jaw, as in *Presbyornis* and ducks, and a tongue accommodated by the lower jaw, as in flamingos. The choice of the lower jaw taken by flamingos (and by baleen whales convergently) led to a highly specialized feeding apparatus that allowed very little adaptive radiation, restricting flamingos largely to alkaline lakes with algal blooms. By contrast, the anseriform bill is much more versatile, being used not only for filter-feeding, but in the geese for cropping and in some ducks for seizing fish.

What we know about *Presbyornis* and its paleoenvironment allows us to reconstuct hypothetical stages that may have occurred in the evolution of modern ducks and modern flamingos. The habitat of *Presbyornis,* the Green River Lake System of Wyoming and Utah, underwent dramatic changes over geological time that presented highly

The first articulated skull of *Presbyornis,* recovered in 1977 from the Canyon Creek butte by Storrs L. Olson and Robert J. Emry. The slightly upturned bill is not an artifact of preservation; all of the many bills now recovered exhibit the same recurved characteristic. The area indicated by the arrow is, however, an artifact of preservation: the bill is actually solid. (From Feduccia, 1978; photo by Victor E. Krantz.)

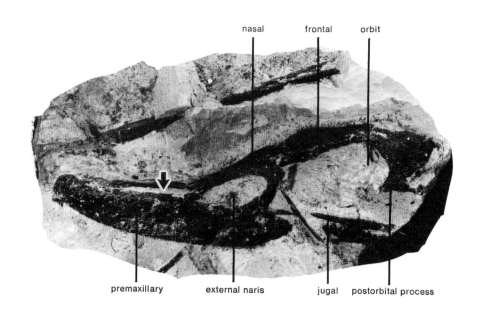

variable selective forces. This lake system came into existence in the early Eocene and occupied thousands of square miles. During a period known as the Wilkins Peak regression, the water in the area became very saline, and vast amounts of trona, or natron, a white or yellowish-white hydrated form of sodium carbonate, were deposited. This suggests that the environment was very much like that of the lakes of East Africa's Rift Valley, the only place where trona is being deposited in large quantities today. Like the most primitive living ducks, *Presbyornis* filter-fed primarily on the large algal blooms and other vegetable matter of alkaline lakes. In contrast, primitive flamingos, like the modern greater flamingo, fed mostly on animal matter. Thus the restricted environment of the Green River area gave rise to two different types of filter-feeders.

The fundamentally different types of filter-feeding apparatus that evolved in the two shorebird lineages leading to flamingos and ducks. The more highly specialized type found in flamingos (above) accommodates the tongue in the lower jaw. The less specialized anseriform feeding apparatus, shown here as a swan's beak (below), accommodates the tongue in the upper jaw, as in *Presbyornis*. (From Lucas and Stettenheim, 1972; courtesy of Alfred M. Lucas.)

A block of the highly resistant (almost concretelike) matrix from the Canyon Creek locality, showing the dense concentrations of *Presbyornis* bones. A modern flamingo lake in the East African Rift Valley could easily produce similar concentrations of bones by normal attrition. (Photo by the author.)

Tracks and dabble marks made by *Presbyornis* 50 million years ago in a Utah Green River Formation lake shore or mudflat. Note that the hind toe touched the ground. (Courtesy of Bruce R. Erickson.)

Presbyornis was highly colonial; the enormous Canyon Creek butte has literally thousands of bones protruding from its coarse sandstones, showing that *Presbyornis* flocked in numbers comparable to those seen today in the flamingo lakes of East Africa. In another locality north of the Canyon Creek butte, large numbers of *Presbyornis* fossils have been found along with an abundance of eggshells, indicating that a large nesting colony existed near the shoreline of a lake. The fossil of a probable predator on *Presbyornis* chicks has also been found, the frigatebird *Limnofregata azygosternon,* a Green River bird that, like *Presbyornis,* could not have been properly identified without the discovery of an associated skeleton (Olson, 1977b).

Fossils also provide evidence that a tropical climate characterized most of North America in the Eocene. Abundant remains of tropical plants, including palm trees, litter the lake deposits, as do the remains of crocodiles and soft-shelled turtles. Some other important finds are the more than 35 species of fossil fish that have been recovered from the Laney Shale and Tipton Tongue of the Green River Formation. Most of these are marine derivatives, and include a ray, herrings (especially *Knightia*), and a number of primitive perchlike species. However, primary freshwater species also have been found, fish that have no tolerance for any salinity, including three species of strictly freshwater catfishes and a gar that probably gained access to the Eocene

Reconstruction of the early Eocene frigatebird *Limnofregata azygosternon,* which probably preyed on the chicks of *Presbyornis*. (From Olson, 1977b; drawing by Anne Curtis.)

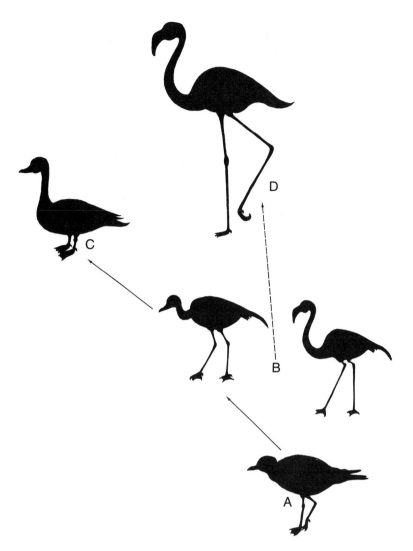

A hypothetical family tree illustrating the probable lineages in the evolution of modern ducks and flamingos. *A* represents the ancestral Cretaceous shorebird stock. To the left of *B* appears the fossil *Presbyornis*. Basically, *Presbyornis* has shorebird limb bones and a skull and bill approximating those of modern ducks in many features. *Presbyornis,* or a form that resembled *Presbyornis* in many ways, was a precursor of modern ducks, and may have been the actual duck ancestor. In the line leading to modern flamingos (*D*), a shorebird prior to *Presbyornis* became differently modified for filter-feeding, with decurvature of the bill, expansion of the lower jaw to accommodate the tongue, and concomitant great increase in leg length for wading. The dotted line indicates that modern flamingos were derived before the time of *Presbyornis,* and from a stiltlike prototype like that shown to the right of *B*. In the line leading to modern ducks, *C*, the legs became shortened and modified for swimming, but the skull changes were only slight, with the upper jaw accommodating the tongue, as in *Presbyornis*; and of course there was change in the nasal region. (Adapted from Feduccia, 1977; original illustration copyright 1977 by Academic Press, Inc., London.)

lakes by freshwater connections. We know from geological evidence that the Green River Lakes underwent major changes in size and in the position of shorelines and deltas; obviously, they must also have varied from being highly saline to being entirely freshwater.

From what we know of the ancient Green River System and of the modern Rift Valley, it is not difficult to imagine the scenario in which flamingos could have evolved. The essential elements are highly colonial stiltlike shorebirds occurring on ancient lakes with the unstable salinity of those of the Green River System. Strong selective forces would have favored the evolution of long legs modified for wading into deeper water and, eventually, along with a myriad of other adaptations, the perfection of a suction filter-feeding mechanism that required great modification of the lower jaw to accommodate the large suction tongue of flamingos. This lineage is indicated on the chart shown above by the dotted line. To the right of *B* appears the hypothetical ancestor, a stiltlike bird that diverged from ancient shorebird stock before the advent of *Presbyornis*. No doubt through various inter-

The Australian freckled duck (*Sticton-etta naevosa*), a primitive anseriform sharing characteristics with both the dabbling ducks and the geese. Interestingly, the structure of the bill of *Stictonetta* is the closest match for that of *Presbyornis* among the living anseriforms (Olson and Feduccia, 1980b). (Drawing by Sigrid K. James, after Frith, 1967.)

mediate forms, this prototype eventually gave rise to modern flamingos.

Obviously, though, the great variety of feeding zones provided by the fluctuating lakes of the Eocene led also to different diversifications of the feeding apparatus. Adaptations leading toward ducks were surely favored in many circumstances. *Presbyornis* already had a duck-like bill, and with only minor modifications it could have diverged to give rise to the beak of modern anseriforms. We can easily imagine also that some lakes had very narrow shorelines, and in such situations it would have been advantageous for *Presbyornis* or a *Presbyornnis*-like bird to begin to perfect swimming adaptations leading to a duck prototype. Alteration from *Presbyornis* to anseriform structure would involve mainly shortening of the leg bones to yield a limb with a more efficient swimming stroke.

The first supposed duck, *Eonessa,* was identified upon unreliable elements, two fragmentary wing bones from the Eocene of North America. The first trustworthy duck fossils are from the Oligocene, about 10 million years later in the middle Tertiary. Duck bones are the most common avian fossils found in the relatively recent North American Pliocene and Pleistocene, showing that they are easily preserved. Therefore, the lack of early Tertiary anseriform fossils could well indicate that ducks and their allies may have originated in the middle Tertiary, after the Eocene Period. *Presbyornis,* as we have seen, embodies many of the morphological features that one would associate with the ancestry of modern ducks, and it occurs in the Eocene, probably before the actual transitions occurred. Even though *Presbyornis* was somewhat specialized for a particular mode of life, there is really nothing in morphology or time to preclude it from the actual ancestry of modern anseriform birds.

Although difficult to trace, the various lineages of modern birds descended from ancient shorebird stock are probably legion. Most of the late Cretaceous fossil birds represented by single elements that do not belong to the hesperornithiform birds are ancient shorebirds, and some, such as *Telmatornis,* are strikingly similar to the living shorebirds of the genus *Burhinus* (Cracraft, 1972). The several species of *Telmatornis,* all from the late Cretaceous of New Jersey, coexisted

The American plain chachalaca (*Ortalis vetula*), one of the 240 species of the order Galliformes (chickens and allies). The galliform birds have been thought by some to be allied with the ducks and geese through the screamers. However, other authors ally them with the hawks and falcons, and the issue remains in dispute. Divided among six well-marked families, galliforms are all terrestrial or semiterrestrial birds, with strong legs adapted for running and short, rounded wings that make them strong fliers for short distances. The oldest galliform fossil of any interest is a nearly complete skeleton from the Eocene of Wyoming known as *Gallinuloides* that is thought to show some resemblance to the chachalacas and the guans (Cracidae). (Drawing by Yvonne Lee.)

The black-necked screamer (*Chauna chavaria*) of northern Colombia and Venezuela. The screamers represent a very aberrant offshoot of the anseriforms, and exhibit only a trace of webbing in the feet. Thought by some to be an anseriform link with the galliforms because of bill structure, the screamers are no doubt highly derived descendants of an ancient form resembling the Australian magpie goose (*Anseranas*), as is illustrated by the presence in the screamer's jaw of vestiges of lamellae, anseriform structures used for filter-feeding (see Olson and Feduccia, 1980b). Screamers are strong fliers, and the wings are "armed" with two sharp and very large spurs. Living in marshes and wet grasslands, screamers feed exclusively on water plants. (Photo by the author, Berlin Zoo.)

A modern shorebird, the blacksmith plover (*Hoplopterus aramatus*), of the family Charadriidae; here pictured at Ngorongoro Crater in Tanzania. (Photo by the author.)

Silhouettes of a sandgrouse (Columbiformes, Pteroclidae), left, and a cursor (Charadriiformes, Glareolidae), right. The columbiform sandgrouse lead by way of the cursors back to shorebird stock. This sequence is carefully documented by Jon Fjeldså (1976). (Drawings by Sigrid K. James.)

with a fairly diverse avifauna, indicating an early divergence of many orders of birds. The shorebirds (Charadriiformes) quickly diversified and are today represented by some 305 species in 16 families falling roughly into three groups: the true shorebirds, such as sandpipers and plovers; the skuas, gulls, and terns; and the auks, murres, and puffins.

The order Gruiformes (cranes, rails, and similar marsh-dwelling waders) is clearly the order closest to the Charadriiformes, and the two orders probably shared a common ancestor derived from ancient shorebird stock. In addition to the 200 or so living species of gruiforms, classified in 12 extremely diverse families, ancient gruiforms gave rise to many other birds, both living and extinct. As we will see in Chapter 6, gruiforms gave rise at several different times to carnivorous, flightless birds, and possibly to some of the ratites, including the ostrich. Additional shorebird derivatives include the sandgrouse, doves, and pigeons (Columbiformes), and, through the toothed-billed pigeons, the parrots (Psittaciformes).

The thought is highly speculative, but there is really nothing to preclude a shorebird ancestry for the petrels and allies (Procellariiformes) and perhaps the pelicans and allies (Pelecaniformes). And, as

A
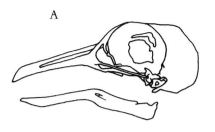

B
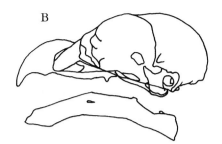

C
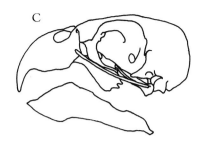

we saw in Chapter 4, the primitive early Eocene tropic bird *Prophaethon* shows a number of shorebird as well as procellariiform features. Indeed, the shorebirds may well be comparable in many respects to the evolutionarily prolific mammalian insectivores in their evolutionary meanderings.

The only large group of waterbirds that shows no evidence of shorebird beginnings is the order Ciconiiformes, with which some avian paleontologists once connected the flamingos. A heterogeneous group of waders living in marshlands or shallow waters, these birds include the storks (Ciconiidae), the herons and bitterns (Ardeidae), the ibises and spoonbills (Threskiornithidae), and two aberrant African forms, the hammerhead (Scopidae) and the whalebill (Balaenicipitidae). Although these groups have few specific characteristics in common, they are all long-necked, long-legged birds with somewhat rounded wings and comparatively short tails; most have long, spreading toes that are sometimes slightly webbed. The sexes are usually identical or quite similar in plumage. One of the few morphological characteristics that unites these birds is a particular conformation of the bones of the palate, in which the palatine bones are fused to each other along the midline of the skull; but this arrangement is also found in a vast array of other birds.

The family of storks is represented by 17 species that occur throughout most of the warmer regions of the world. Those that nest in the temperate zone migrate great distances to reach their wintering grounds. Storks differ in many ways from other ciconiiform birds, and have been shown by David Ligon (1967) to share many features with the New World vultures (Cathartidae), including the habit of cooling the body by excreting liquid uric acid on the legs. Storks have rather short toes that are partially webbed at the base, and because they lack muscles in the voice box, storks are mute and communicate by rattling their bills. There are fossil storks from as long ago as the early Oligocene or Eocene of France, but they tell us nothing of the relationships of the Ciconiidae. Storks do, however, possess a distinctive tubular ear bone (Feduccia, 1977a) that is otherwise found in the whalebill and, in modified form, in the hammerhead, but this bone does not differ greatly from the ear bone of the pelecaniform birds.

Skulls of: (*A*) a ground dove (*Gallicolumba*), (*B*) the Samoan tooth-billed pigeon (*Didunculus strigirostris*), and (*C*) a parrot, the lory *Trichglossus.* The skull of the tooth-billed pigeon (*B*) exhibits structural trends toward parrots; these similarities favor the view, supported by other parts of the skeleton, that the doves and pigeons (Columbiformes) are the order most closely related to the parrots (Psittaciformes), and that parrots are columbiform derivatives. The tooth-billed pigeons are probably surviving relicts of a group that became specialized after diverging from the main stem of columbiform evolution, and they show many anatomical features that would be found in the ancestral stock of parrots. (Drawing by Sigrid K. James, after Burton, 1974.)

The tubular middle-ear bone shared by storks, whalebills (*Balaeniceps*) and, in modified form, by hammerheads. (Drawing by Linda M. Hillowe.)

The marabou stork (*Leptoptilos crumeniferus*), shown on the Serengeti Plains. The marabou is among the world's largest living birds. In addition to capturing live prey, including flamingos, marabous also eat carrion. (Photos by the author.)

The whalebill (*Balaeniceps rex*). The large bill is apparently adapted for feeding on lungfish in the murky waters of African marshes. (Photo by the author, Berlin Zoo.)

The enigmatic African hammerhead (*Scopus umbretta*), thought to be related in some way to both storks and the whalebill. Hammerheads build huge, dome-shaped nests often several yards in diameter, with a compartmented interior and a small entrance on the least accessible side. (Drawing by Melissa Marshall.)

The curious African whalebill, *Balaeniceps rex*, aside from having a storklike ear bone, is also a bill-rattler. It was regarded by its original describer (John Gould, 1852), as having pelecaniform affinities, and in a detailed paper in 1957 Patricia A. Cottam described several important features of the whalebill that indicate pelecaniform relationships. Recently, Storrs Olson has suggested that the whalebills, hammerheads, and storks "may be loosely interrelated and have affinities with the Pelecaniformes" (1979, p. 169). Regardless of the ultimate ancestry of these birds, it is clear that storks and whalebills share a number of characteristics with the pelecaniform birds.

A sacred ibis (*Threskiornis aethiopica*) at its nest in Kenya. (Photo by the author.)

The affinities of the herons and ibises are another matter. Although there is a supposed ibis fossil from the Paleocene of North Dakota, neither it nor the later fossil ibises that have been recovered tell us anything about either the evolution of ibises or their relationships to other avian groups. Although superficially similar to other ciconiiformes, ibises differ from all other birds in the order in many features. Perhaps their most dramatic departure is their elongated schizorhinal nostrils, characteristic of shorebirds, in which the posterior margin forms a slit. The long, decurved bill of ibises is equipped with sensory pits at the tip, somewhat like those of curlews.

Even more distinctive than ibises are the herons, which show almost no anatomical similarity with the other members of the Ciconiiformes. In addition to having very distinctive bones, herons have a highly unusual pattern of feather arrangement and powderdown patches, like those of some of the primitive gruiform birds. Storrs Olson has recently suggested that herons and bitterns "are the only currently successful group in an early radiation of primitive Gruiformes" (1979, p. 169).

Clearly, we are a long way from understanding the relationships of the various groups currently included within the Ciconiiformes. The phylogenies of these birds are still a major challenge to evolutionary ornithologists.

The black-crowned night heron (*Nycticorax nycticorax*). (Drawing by Yvonne Lee.)

The Evolution of Flightlessness

6

Flight is an energetically expensive ability to maintain, both in terms of metabolism and in terms of embryogenesis. If there is no strong and continual selection for the maintenance of the flight apparatus, then it tends to disappear. In each case the reasons may be quite distinctive, but the evolution of flightlessness is a pervasive phenomenon in birds, in both aquatic and terrestrial groups, on continents as well as islands, in birds as diverse as geese and hoopoes. Flightlessness occurred as early as the foot-propelled Cretaceous divers of Chapter 4, and as late as island rails that have adapted to flightlessness within the past few thousand years. Some flightless birds retain characteristics that tell of their ancestry from a specific avian group; others have become so greatly modified that we are left with no clue as to their origin or their possible interrelatedness. Yet the fact remains that flightlessness as a specific characteristic did evolve, and all flightless forms have been derived from flying predecessors.

At the beginning of the Age of Birds and Mammals, the Cenozoic Era, about 65 million years ago, the niche for a bipedal carnivore had been left vacant by the extinction of the flesh-eating dinosaurs. In the resulting absence of competition, giant, flightless birds adapted for a predatory existence were able to succeed. The oldest of these that we know of were the huge diatrymas (*Diatryma, Gastornis,* and allies), apparently derived from gruiform stock. They are known from both Paleocene and Eocene deposits in Wyoming, New Mexico, and New Jersey, and from Eocene deposits in France and Germany, suggesting a wide distribution facilitated by the Atlantic land bridge that connected Europe and North America until the latter part of the Eocene. The diatrymas were 6 to 7 feet tall, and had massive legs and toes equipped with great claws. The wings were greatly reduced and the sternum was not keeled. The head was titanic, almost as big as a horse's, and the very large and powerful beak easily could have been adapted for tearing flesh. Nonetheless, some authors have argued that the diatrymas were peaceful vegetarians, using their huge beaks for cropping grasses rather than for subduing prey. While this remains a possibility, a recently extinct grazer and cropper, the elephantbird, was much larger than any diatryma and yet had a relatively very small head. In

Skeleton of *Diatryma gigantea* from the early Eocene of New Mexico. (Courtesy of the American Museum of Natural History.)

Restoration of *Diatryma gigantea*. (From Heilmann, 1926.)

addition, as I have noted, the moment in evolutionary history was opportune for an avian flesh-eater. True, the short, stout limb bones of *Diatryma* indicate that it was not a particularly fast runner, but neither were the archaic mammals upon which it probably preyed.

Because of the geographic isolation of South America from advanced mammalian carnivores during most of the Cenozoic Era, another line of flightless birds evolved called the phorusrhacids, typified by the genus *Phorusrhacos* (formerly known as *Phororhacos*). They are known from the Oligocene, 38 million years ago, to the close of the Pliocene, approximately 4 million years ago. Their extinction at that time presumably resulted from the invasion of North American flesh-eating mammals, crossing over the newly established Central American land bridge. The dozen or so species of phorusrhacids (Phorusrhacidae), which also include *Brontornis* and *Andalgalornis,* were rather lightly built but averaged 5 to 8 feet in height. They too were equipped

A restoration of the phorusrhacid *Phorusrhacos* (formerly *Phororhacos*), a giant flightless bird from the Miocene of Patagonia. (Painting by Charles R. Knight; courtesy of the American Museum of Natural History.)

with a powerful hooked beak, highly adapted for tearing flesh, but unlike the diatrymas, these gruiform derivatives undoubtedly were swift enough to run down fast-moving mammals.

During the Pleistocene, the great Ice Age, other giant raptorial, or predatory, birds evolved on the islands of the Antilles to occupy the niches usually filled by carnivorous mammals in continental areas. These forms, belonging to the orders Strigiformes (owls) and Accipitriformes (hawks and eagles), included a giant eagle, a vulture similar in size to the Andean condor, and four giant species of barn owls. Perhaps most spectacular of all was a gigantic flightless owl from Cuba, *Ornimegalonyx oteroi,* probably over 3 feet tall, whose tarsometatarsus measures over twice the length of that of our great horned owl *Bubo virginiensis* (Arredondo, 1976). At the same time, in Florida, there existed a giant phorusrhacid known as *Titanus walleri,* described by Pierce Brodkorb as "larger than the African ostrich and more than twice the

The recently extinct dodo of Mauritius.
(Drawing by Yvonne Lee.)

size of the South American rhea" (1963, p. 111). *Titanus* probably arrived in North America from South America during or slightly before the Ice Age, crossing over the Central American land bridge.

Another distinctive avian order that has given rise to flightless species is the Columbiformes, the pigeons and doves. A familiar flightless columbiform derivative is *Raphus cucullatus,* the dodo of the island of Mauritius, in the Indian Ocean. About the size of a large turkey, the dodo weighed approximately 50 pounds. The species was exterminated at the close of the seventeenth century by newly introduced pigs and monkeys that ate the eggs, and by European sailors who provisioned their merchant ships with the birds. The dodos, whose name is derived from the Portuguese *doudo,* a simpleton, were ill equipped to survive such predation: their clutch consisted of a single egg, laid on the ground, and both parents spent time on the nest.

At almost exactly the same time, a slightly smaller and perhaps less modified flightless cousin of the dodo died out on a neighboring island. This was the Rodriguez solitaire (*Pezophaps solitarius*), last seen alive at the end of the seventeenth century. Both solitaires and dodos were dramatically different from their ancestors in size and other features, and in all probability they were derived from a single columbiform invasion of the Mascarene Islands.

Even today the order Columbiformes has species that show a tendency toward flightlessness, with such semiterrestrial forms as

Reconstruction and skull of the Rodriguez solitaire (*Pezophaps solitarius*). (Solitaire drawing by Melissa Marshall; skull from Simonetta, 1960.)

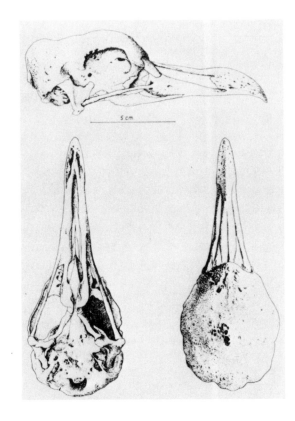

The flightless kakapo, or owl parrot (*Strigops habroptilus*), of New Zealand. Largely nocturnal, it emerges at evening to feed, often climbing trees to get fruit and then gliding down to the ground, where it runs rapidly, frequently spreading its wings. (Drawing by Melissa Marshall.)

the so-called ground pigeons, ground doves, and quail doves. The crowned pigeon (*Goura cristata*) of New Guinea is also semiterrestrial, as is the bleeding-heart pigeon (*Gallicolumba luzonica*) of the Philippines. The columbiforms' close allies, the parrots, include one flightless species, the kakapo, or owl parrot (*Strigops habroptilus*), and one largely terrestrial form, the Australian ground parrot (*Pezoporus wallicus*).

But the birds showing the greatest tendency to become flightless are members of the ancient order Gruiformes, which has given rise not only to the diatrymas and phorusrhacids, but also to many other flightless forms, both living and extinct. As we saw in Chapter 5, the Gruiformes probably shared an ancient common ancestor with the shorebirds. We know for certain that there was an extensive adaptive radiation of gruiform birds in the Eocene and Oligocene, memorialized by a number of flightless and nearly flightless fossil forms. Perhaps best-known of these are the six species of *Bathornis,* large, cursorial ground-dwelling birds that lived in North America. Other fossil gruiforms include the flightless and highly cursorial *Ergilornis* and *Urmiornis,* from the Oligocene of Eurasia, forms that, as we shall see, may have been involved in the ancestry of the ostrich.

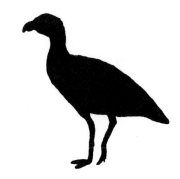

The fossil gruiform *Bathornis,* from the early Oligocene to the early Miocene of North America. (Drawing by Yvonne Lee, after Fisher and Peterson, 1964.)

Today the order Gruiformes is represented by a number of extremely diverse birds, many of them ancient forms. They include the cranes, derived from Eocene fossil lineages that also gave rise to species that became highly cursorial and flightless, and the bustards, large birds that can fly but are mainly cursorial in habit. The ancient mesites of Madagascar are nearly flightless, and the kagu of New Caledonia is a totally flightless form. But the largest and most successful group of living gruiforms is the rails (Rallidae), consisting of 132 species with a nearly cosmopolitan distribution. Of all living birds, the rails are the most likely to develop flightlessness. Almost one-fourth of all island rails, living or recently extinct, have lost the ability to fly; all flightless rails are island forms, although the islands may range in size from tiny, austere Laysan to the large, lush, and topographically diverse islands of New Guinea and New Zealand. Rails thus provide us with a living laboratory for examining the structural changes that occur in the evolution of flightlessness.

The primitive African crowned crane (*Balearica pavonina*) and the sarus crane (*Grus antigone*) of India, Burma, and Thailand. Successful remnants of a diverse adaptive radiation that began in the Eocene, the 14 species of cranes (Gruidae) are one of the most spectacular gruiform families. (Photos by the author.)

The kori bustard (*Choriotis kori*) of the gruiform family Otitidae. A cursorial ground bird of the grasslands, it is typical of the 16 species of bustards. Known from the middle Eocene of Germany, bustards are relict gruiforms that resemble the ratites in many features, particularly in the chicks. They are thought to be allied with two living species of South American relict gruiforms, the seriemas (Cariamidae), which have nearly identical cestode parasites. Seriemas are also cursorial ground birds. (Photo by the author, Serengeti Plains.)

Mesoenas variegata, one of the three species of the primitive Malagasy gruiforms, the mesites. Nearly flightless,
these birds live in the brushlands and
forests of Madagascar, where they nor-
mally walk or run, but seldom, if ever,
fly. They reach their nests by climbing,
not flying. All have greatly reduced
clavicles and powderdown, features not
found in any other members of the
Gruiformes. (Drawing by Sigrid K.
James, after Brasil, 1914.)

The flightless kagu (*Rhynochetos ju-
batus*), a gruiform from New Caledonia. (From Van Tyne and Berger,
1976; drawing by George Miksch Sutton.)

The weka (*Gallirallus australis*), a flightless New Zealand wood rail about
the size of a small chicken. (Drawing
by Sigrid K. James, after Austin, 1961.)

The now extinct Mascarene Island
flightless rail (*Aphanapteryx leguati*); it
disappeared from Rodriguez in the seventeenth century. (Drawing by Melissa
Marshall.)

The Virginia rail (*Rallus limicola*), a volant species of the Western Hemisphere. (Drawing by Yvonne Lee.)

When a bird becomes flightless, it undergoes dramatic modification. The major change is the immediate reduction of the muscles and
bones of the wing and pectoral girdle. The keel of the sternum is
greatly reduced or lost, along with the loss of flight muscles. Because
the body no longer needs to be lightened for flying, most flightless
birds have a decided tendency to become large. So, as birds are structurally similar in possessing the ability to fly, they become structurally
similar in the loss of flight.

Many of these adaptations help the flightless bird save energy. Among the first features to disappear are the expensive flight muscles, especially the pectoralis. The flight muscles alone account for as much as 17 percent of the total body weight of most birds, and the entire flight apparatus, including muscles and bones of the pectoral girdle and sternum, averages 20–25 percent of body weight in typical birds. It is not just the loss of bulk that decreases energy output; flight muscles require an inordinate amount of energy to maintain, so any reduction in them immediately confers great advantage in energy savings.

Reduction or loss of the sternal and flight apparatus generally comes about through arrested development, or neoteny; and flightless birds, as well as those with a strong tendency to become flightless, are characterized by a number of neotenic features. Whenever arrested development affects a particular part of an organism, we see similar effects in other structures and organs. Indeed, development can only be arrested without lethal consequences after essential organs have developed sufficiently to sustain life.

Particularly interesting here is the late development of the sternum in rails, pigeons, and grebes, groups that have given rise to flightless forms in numerous instances. It has long been known that ossification of the sternum does not occur until after hatching in domestic pigeons, *Columba livia,* and the grebe *Podiceps cristata* (Schinz and Zangrel, 1937), and Storrs Olson (1973) has recently shown that the same is true for rails. As long as 17 days after hatching, when all other major bones are relatively well ossified, the king rail (*Rallus elegans*) still has only a cartilaginous outline of the sternum, and at 47 days the sternum is only beginning to ossify. It is this postponed development of the sternal apparatus that allows neoteny in rails to result in the loss of the flight apparatus without also resulting in the loss of the rail.

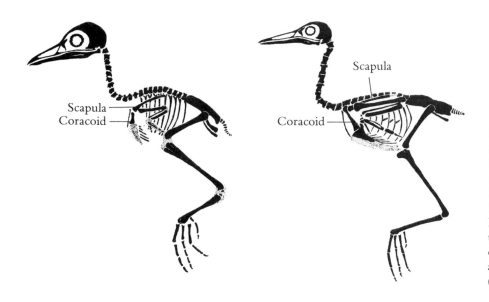

Cleared and stained skeletons of the king rail (*Rallus elegans*), a flying rail: (left) at 17 days after hatching; (right) at 47 days (reduced so that the femur lengths in the two drawings are equal). Stippled areas represent cartilage. Note the obtuse angle formed by the articulation of the scapula and coracoid in the younger form, the acute angle in the older form. (From Olson, 1973.)

Development of the sternum of the flying rail *Porphyrula martinica* (*a, c, e*), showing how the carina in its early stages corresponds to the shape of the carina in two different species of flightless rails (*b, d*). (*a*) *P. martinica,* downy chick about a week old; the sternum is entirely cartilaginous but has nearly the same conformation as *b.* (*b*) *Gallirallus australis,* a flightless rail, adult. (*c*) *P. martinica,* an immature that is fully feathered but not quite volant; the sternum is still partly cartilaginous and now resembles *d.* (*d*) *Gallirallus owstoni,* a flightless rail, adult. (*e*) *P. martinica,* adult. The scales equal 5 millimeters. Dotted lines indicate cartilage. (From Olson, 1973.)

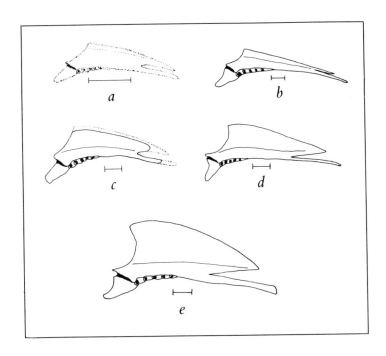

Chicks of the clapper rail (*Rallus longirostris*), left, and the great curassow (*Crax rubra*), a galliform, right, represent the two extremes in relative development of the pectoral flight apparatus of the downy young. Rails, born with essentially no development of the sternal keel and associated flight apparatus, can easily arrest development and give rise to flightless species. Galliform birds, by contrast, are endowed with nearly fully developed flight machinery at birth. For them to give rise to flightless species, development would have to be arrested far in advance of hatching, when other organs have not yet developed, and the results might well be lethal. (Left: adapted from Ripley, 1977; right: adapted from Delacour and Amadon, 1973.)

By contrast, birds such as the Galliformes (chickens and allies) that develop the sternal apparatus very late have never given rise to flightless forms. Galliforms are among the strongest fliers for short distances. In the domestic fowl, a typical galliform, the major bones of the sternum begin to ossify between the eighth and twelfth days of incubation, rather than after hatching, so that the chick has almost fully developed flight capacity at birth. Galliforms probably could never survive arrested development of the sternal apparatus that would occur early enough to rid them of the keeled sternum.

It should be clear by now that the keelless sternum is characteristic of birds that have become flightless and can therefore provide no evidence for evolutionary relationships between avian groups. The flat-bottomed sternum has been used to ally the flightless ostriches, kiwis, emus, rheas, and cassowaries into a single assemblage called ratites

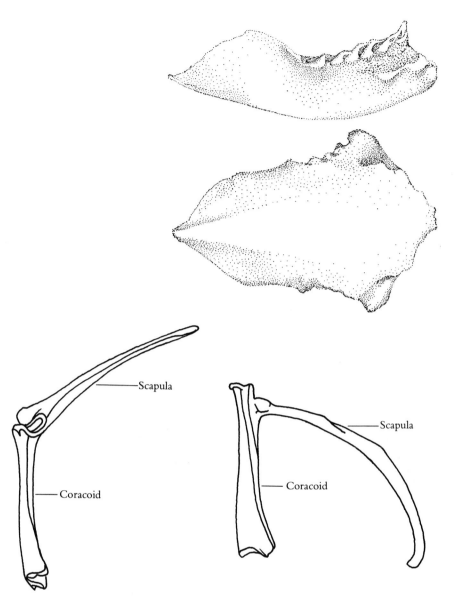

Lateral view (above) and ventral view (below) of the sternum of a cassowary, illustrating the lack of a keel characteristic of the ratites. (Drawing by Yvonne Lee.)

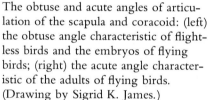

The obtuse and acute angles of articulation of the scapula and coracoid: (left) the obtuse angle characteristic of flightless birds and the embryos of flying birds; (right) the acute angle characteristic of the adults of flying birds. (Drawing by Sigrid K. James.)

(from the Latin *ratis*, meaning raft), but the keeled sternum is absent also not only in *Hesperornis*, but in flightless rails, an extinct flightless goose, a flightless ibis from Hawaii, and a flightless gruiform from New Zealand. And the keel has almost disappeared from the flightless grebe of Lake Titicaca, the flightless Galápagos cormorant, and the nearly flightless Central American passerine *Zeledonia*.

Another anatomical feature that predictably changes with flightlessness is the angle of articulation between the coracoid and scapula. In flying birds, as we saw in Chapter 3, this angle is acute; an acute angle shortens the distance through which the dorsal elevators must act, thus providing greater power. When flightlessness occurs, the angle exceeds 90°, and in the large flightless ratites the two bones meet in an extremely obtuse angle and fuse to form a single scapulocoracoid, quite similar to that found in many dinosaurs.

First recognized by T. H. Huxley as a characteristic of flightless birds, the obtuse angle of the scapula-coracoid articulation is also neotenic in birds, as shown by the development of the skeleton in rails in the figure on page 111. The angle of the articulation decreases as the sternum enlarges along with the pectoral muscle mass. Flightless rails retain the neotenic obtuse angle of the scapula-coracoid articulation, and in the recently extinct Hawaiian goose, *Thambetochen chauliodous* (described by Olson and Wetmore, 1976), the angle is so obtuse as to approach the ratite condition, although the two bones are not fused. The Hawaiian goose had a keelless sternum and also lacked clavicles, just as does the ostrich. It was a big gosling—a striking case of arrested development.

Still another characteristic of adult ratites that is seen in the embryos of rails and other modern birds is the broad unossified region

Life reconstruction of the extinct Hawaiian flightless goose (*Thambetochen chauliodous*), known from the Pleistocene. (Painting by Dr. H. Douglas Pratt; courtesy of the Bernice P. Bishop Museum.)

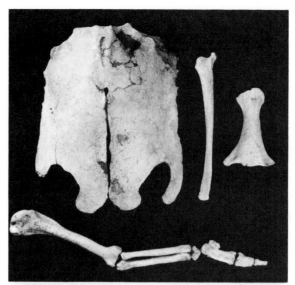

Fossil bones of *Thambetochen chauliodous*. Left to right and top to bottom: sternum (note lack of keel), scapula, coracoid, right wing (note drastic reduction), femur, tibiotarsus, and tarsometatarsus. Note that the bones have come to resemble convergently those of the large ratites in loss of the sternal keel, reduction of the wing to a vestige, and the greatly increased size of the leg bones. (From Olson and Wetmore, 1976; photo by Victor E. Krantz.)

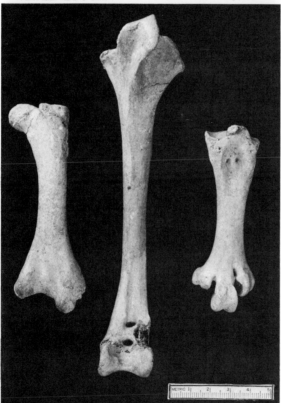

The rostrum of *Thambetochen chauliodous*. Note the blunt, bony, toothlike projections; they are also present on the lower jaw. (From Olson and Wetmore, 1976; photo by Victor E. Krantz.)

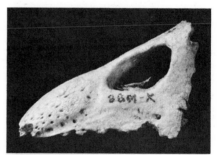

between the ilium and ischium in the pelvic region, known as the ilioschiatic fenestra. This condition, also found as a primitive state in *Archaeopteryx, Hesperornis,* and *Ichthyornis,* is surely neotenic in living flightless birds. Another neotenic feature seen in the embryos of today's flying birds and in the adults of some ratites, such as the ostrich, is skull sutures, rather than the extensively fused skull bones characteristic of adult flying birds.

How much time is necessary for flying birds to lose their volant powers has been a subject of some controversy. In the past it has often been thought that vast time spans were required—tens of millions of years perhaps; but it now seems more likely that the evolution of flightlessness and the concomitant attainment of large size, as seen dramatically in the ratites, needs relatively little time, especially on islands.

Once again, the rails provide telling evidence. Storrs Olson has pointed out that "the span of time needed to evolve flightlessness in rails can probably be measured in generations rather than in millennia" (1973, p. 34). This generalization is bolstered by the occurrence of two nearly identical flightless rails 250 miles apart on Tristan da Cunha and on Gough Island, the gallinules *Gallinula nesiotis* and *G. comeri,* respectively. They are perhaps best treated as subspecies or sibling species

Life reconstruction of the flightless Hawaiian ibis (*Apteribis glenos*). Shown with it are two extinct flightless rails. (Painting by Dr. H. Douglas Pratt; courtesy of the Bernice P. Bishop Museum.)

(similar populations that have become reproductively isolated) of the modern common gallinule (*Gallinula chloropus*), and are therefore of only very recent origin. In addition, there are flying and flightless races in a single rail species, *Dryolimnus cuvieri*; and a completely flightless rail, *Atlantisia elpenor,* is present on Ascension, an island whose oldest rocks have been dated at only 1.5 million years.

We do not know how long it would take for these forms to become unrecognizable as rails through the evolution of gigantism or bizarre adaptations. But we need only look at the flightless ibis *Apteribis*, discovered in Pleistocene deposits in Hawaii, to see how modifications for flightlessness can disguise a bird's ancestry. "The hindlimb . . . is so modified from that of typical ibises as almost to defy identification. At first we had only the femur, tibiotarsus, and tarsometatarsus to work with, and of all modern birds the proportions of these elements most closely approached those of the kiwis . . . and it was not until we received the associated material from Maui . . . that our suspicions were confirmed" (Olson and Wetmore, 1976, pp. 250–251). Had it not become extinct, what might *Apteribis* have looked like in another million years?

Of all flightless birds, however, none has received more attention than the living ratites and their supposed relatives, the extinct elephantbirds of Madagascar and the moas of New Zealand. These extinct forms, known only from the Pleistocene and Recent sites, provide additional evidence that not only flightlessness but gigantism as well can occur in a very short period of time. Both birds evolved to fill a grazing niche on their respective islands that was never occupied by a mammalian herbivore. Unlike the ostriches, rheas, and emus, which evolved great speed in running as an adaptation for eluding predators in open continental areas, these island forms evolved great size and adaptations for a graviportal locomotion to support their ponderous

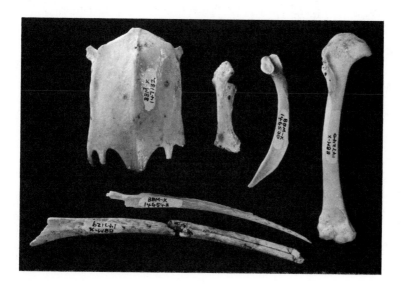

Fossil bones of *Apteribis glenos.* Left to right and top to bottom: sternum (note lack of keel), coracoid, scapula, humerus (note reduced size), fragment of rostrum, and two fragments of mandible. (From Olson and Wetmore, 1976; photo by Victor E. Krantz.)

A restoration of giant moas (*Dinornis*) on the South Island of New Zealand during postglacial times (5,000 years ago). Dean Amadon (1947) estimated that the largest moa, *Dinornis maximus*, weighed 520 pounds and, at 10 to 12 feet in height, was the tallest bird known to have lived. The evidence from moa-hunter camps indicates that most of the moas, and possibly all except several small forms, had become extinct before the arrival of man. (Painting by Charles R. Knight; courtesy of the Field Museum of Natural History, Chicago.)

weight. They had a short, stocky tarsometatarsus with short, heavy toes splayed out to form a broad and stable foot, obviously associated with walking, not with rapid locomotion.

The moas, which superficially resemble large, flightless geese, were a diversified group, mostly confined to the North and South Islands of New Zealand. For a time, they coexisted with the native Maori, who arrived in New Zealand about 1,000 years ago and gave these strange birds their name. The first published accounts of the moas are from a narrative of the early explorer J. S. Polack, who traveled in that country between 1831 and 1837: "That a species of the emu, or bird of the genus *Struthio*, formerly existed in the [North] island I feel well assured, as several fossil ossifications were shewn to me when I was residing in the vicinity of the East Cape, said to have been found at the base of the inland mountain of Ikorangi . . . The natives added that, in times long past they received the tradition that very

Reconstruction of a small moa (*Euryapteryx*). (Courtesy of the American Museum of Natural History.)

large birds had existed, but the scarcity of animal food, as well as the easy method of entrapping them, had caused their extermination" (1838, p. 303). Later on Polack writes: "Petrifactions of the bones of large birds supposed to be wholly extinct have often been presented to me by the natives . . . Many of the petrifactions have been the ossified parts of birds, that are at present (as far as is known) extinct in these islands, whose probable tameness, or want of volitary powers, caused them to be early extirpated by a people, driven by both hunger and superstition (either reason is quite sufficient in its way) to rid themselves of their presence" (1838, pp. 345, 346).

The first bone of a moa, a femur shaft, to be viewed by a scientist arrived in England in 1839 and was carefully studied by Sir Richard Owen, who at first doubted that any bird could have a bone so large or that such a bird bone could have come from New Zealand. The femur that he observed, that of the largest moa, was larger than the femur of an ostrich. But eventually Owen became convinced that a giant, extinct bird had once inhabited New Zealand, and he gave it the generic name *Dinornis*. Later, when Europeans began to explore New Zealand thoroughly, they found bones of moas exposed on the surface of the ground in great profusion, particularly in caves and swamps. Bones were also found in association with old Maori cooking places, often showing traces of scorching. Where conditions were particularly favorable for preservation, skeletons have been found with stomach contents, ligaments, and even feathers. Small forms of the moa were common, but the very large species appear to have been relatively rare.

The many genera and species identified since the original description by Owen were summarized by W. R. B. Oliver (1949), but they have remained a taxonomic nightmare until recently, when Joel Cracraft (1976) systematically studied them. He concluded that approximately 5 genera and 13 species existed, divisible into two groups, the greater and lesser moas. They ranged in size from the giant moas (*Dinornis*), some possibly having stood 10 feet high or more, to the small forms, some about the size of a large turkey, each apparently adapted for grazing or browsing in a different way.

Our extensive knowledge of moas comes from the many fossils that are preserved in the extraordinary swamps of New Zealand, where moas apparently became bogged down by their great weight. In one of these swamps, it is estimated that 800 individual birds were packed into an area no more than 30 by 20 feet, and 10 feet deep. But the most remarkable of all is the Pyramid Valley Moa Swamp, discovered in North Canterbury on the South Island in 1937. Five years after its discovery, no less than 50 fairly complete skeletons had been excavated from the $3\frac{1}{2}$-acre swamp, and by 1949, 140 specimens had been removed (Duff, 1949). Among them were 44 specimens of the large *Dinornis,* from 10 to 12 feet tall; 14 skeletons of *Pachyornis,* from $5\frac{1}{2}$ to 7 feet tall; and 12 specimens of *Euryapteryx,* from $4\frac{1}{2}$ to $5\frac{1}{2}$ feet tall. There were 70 specimens of *Emeus,* about the size of *Euryapteryx.* (*Pachyornis* and *Euryapteryx* are somewhat different from the other moas in having very short and relatively massive legs.) Many of these fossils have been found in upright stance with all of the bones articulated.

It has been estimated that as many as 800 birds per acre are preserved at Pyramid Valley. Along with the moas, excavators found a number of other flightless birds, including the flightless New Zealand gallinule, or takahe (*Notornis*), a large flightless gruiform bird (*Aptornis*), and a large flightless goose (*Cnemiornis*). These birds shared the wealth of New Zealand's shrubs and grasses in the absence of grazing mammals. The flightless kiwi (*Apteryx*) is also preserved at Pyramid Valley.

Aside from the usual features associated with flightlessness, including a keelless sternum, large size, and an open pelvic region, moas shared few characters with the other ratites except the palaeognathous palate, discussed later on. In contrast to the living ratites, the moas had no wings and no pygostyle, and they were equipped with a tendonal canal in the distal end of the tibia, a feature present in flying birds but not in other ratites. Owing to the remarkably well-preserved fossils, we know that the feathers of moas had a well-developed aftershaft, as in the living cassowaries. Large numbers of "gizzard stones" for grinding food, some as large as several inches across, have been found associated with many skeletons.

The moas show that herbivory can be achieved through the evolution of flightlessness. True herbivory, confined to the parrots, the

Skull of a moa (*Anomalopteryx didiformis*). (From Simonetta, 1960.)

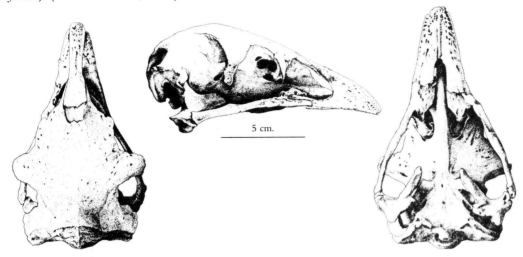

5 cm.

Skeleton of the large flightless gruiform *Aptornis*. (From Andrews, 1896.)

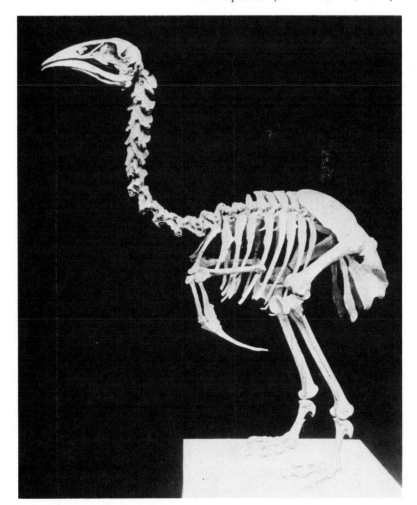

The flightless New Zealand gallinule (*Notornis mantelli*), known to the Maoris as the takahe, is the size of a small turkey. First described from a fossil skull in 1848 by Sir Richard Owen, and at that time thought to be extinct, it was discovered alive a few years later, and the living bird turned out to be distinctive from the fossil species. In 1948, nearly a century after the last live bird had been collected, a small population, now thought to number about 100 individuals, was discovered in several remote valleys on New Zealand's South Island. (Drawing by Melissa Marshall.)

South American hoatzin, and several other isolated forms, is extremely rare in birds, because in a flying animal the weight of a long caecum, the intestinal appendage necessary to house bacteria to digest cellulose, cannot usually be tolerated. But once birds become flightless, the added weight of the caecum is easily accommodated.

While the Pleistocene radiation of moas in New Zealand produced the tallest bird, the heaviest, the elephantbird, evolved during the same era on the island of Madagascar. In the thirteenth century, Marco Polo recorded that the legendary roc came from Madagascar. This part of the roc tale may not have been so legendary, but if Sinbad the Sailor was borne off by huge flying birds, the elephantbird cannot be blamed; it was wholly earthbound.

The seven species of elephantbirds, some the size of a cassowary, were still present less than 2,000 years ago, when man arrived on Madagascar. Radiocarbon dates of eggshell fragments (Burger et al., 1975)

The largest of the elephantbirds (*Aepyornis maximus*), which probably weighed close to 1,000 pounds. (Drawing by Sigrid K. James, after Wetmore, 1967.)

Skull of an elephantbird (*Aepyornis hildebrandti*). (From Simonetta, 1960.)

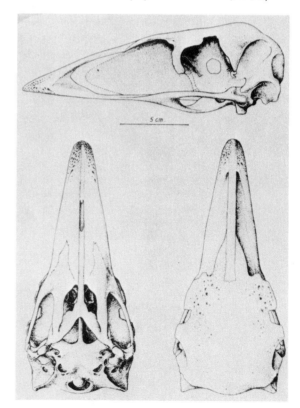

5 cm

indicate that the birds were widespread as late as the tenth century. Their extinction probably took place gradually over many centuries, because they had no major enemies—the only large predator on Madagascar, until man arrived, was the crocodile. Under these conditions, the adaptive radiation of elephantbirds produced a variety of species, but only one attained elephantine proportions, *Aepyornis maximus* ("largest tall bird"). This ponderous giant with elephant-style legs stood 9 to 10 feet tall, and Dean Amadon (1947) of the American Museum of Natural History in New York has calculated that its weight was close to 1,000 pounds. By contrast, a large ostrich may attain a height of 8 feet and weigh about 300 pounds. Like the moas of New Zealand, the elephantbirds were grazers, and probably, as the late Alexander Wetmore (1967) noted, they also cropped the lower branches of shrubs and trees, which they could easily reach with their long necks. Somewhat similar to moas in their graviportal posture, the elephantbirds differed from them in having vestigial wings and a pygostyle.

The elephantbird is first mentioned in a book by the French traveler E. de Flacourt in 1661, but the most vivid early descriptions appear in the diary of a Mr. Joliffe, surgeon of H.M.S. *Geyser,* which was cruising off Madagascar in October 1848 with a French merchant, M. Dumarele, on board.

> M. Dumarele casually mentioned that some time previously, when in command of his own vessel trading along the coasts of Madagascar, he saw at Port Liven, on the North-west end of the island, the shell of an enormous egg, the production of an unknown bird inhabiting the wilds of the country which held the incredible quantity of *13 wine quart bottles of fluid!!!* he having himself carefully measured the quantity. It was of the colour and appearance of an ostrich egg, and the substance of the shell was about the thickness of a spanish dollar, and very hard in texture. It was brought on board by the natives (the race of "Sakalavas") to be filled with rum, having a tolerably large hole at one end through which the contents of the egg had been extracted, and which served as the mouth of the vessel. M. Dumarele offered to purchase the egg from the natives, but they declined selling it, stating that it belonged to their chief, and that they could not dispose of it without his permission. The natives said the egg was found in the jungle, and observed that such eggs were *very very rarely* met with, and that the bird which produces them is still more rarely seen.   (Strickland, 1849, pp. 338–339)

Many eggs have now been recovered, some weighing more than 20 pounds, measuring over a foot in length, and equal in volume to seven ostrich eggs. One actually contains an embryo, revealed by x-rays. The eggs of *Aepyornis* are the largest birds' eggs known, and as Josselyn Van Tyne and Andrew J. Burger (1976) have noted, "such an egg would hold the contents of seven ostrich eggs or 183 chicken eggs or more than 12,000 hummingbird eggs."

The provable fossil record of elephantbirds is confined to the Pleistocene and Recent remains known from Madagascar, but this has not stopped paleontologists from assigning fragmentary material to the elephantbirds. Two pieces of leg bones from the Fayum of Egypt, a region south of Cairo, have been identified on totally insufficient grounds as belonging to the Aepyornithiformes, the order containing elephantbirds. One of these is a small fragment of a tibiotarsus in the British Museum (Natural History) named *Eremopezus,* and the other is a piece of a tarsometatarsus from the Oligocene named *Stromeria.* Even an eggshell fragment, called *Psammornis,* from the Eocene of southern Algeria has been assigned to the elephantbird. Moreover, Franz Sauer (1976) has reported "aepyornithoid" eggshells from the Miocene and Pliocene of Turkey, and Sauer and Peter Rothe (1972) have described shells from Miocene and Pliocene deposits on the Canary Islands as "aepyornithoid." These attributions are based on the shells' relatively large pore size. But pore size increases with egg size, and there is no valid evidence that these specimens are from elephantbirds; all of them could easily be eggshells of other large flightless birds.

In the absence of a reliable fossil record extending beyond the Pleistocene, it is difficult to explain the existence of elephantbirds on Madagascar, an island that has been separated from continental Africa since at least late Cretaceous time. We must postulate either that the elephantbirds are an ancient group that evolved flightlessness in continental Africa, were present on Madagascar at the time of the separation of the two land masses, and subsequently became extinct in continental Africa; or that they are not as ancient as the late Cretaceous and were derived from ancestors that flew to Madagascar and became flightless subsequently. At present, the latter explanation appears more probable.

The first attempt to ally the living ratites was made by T. H. Huxley in 1867. During the subsequent hundred years, controversy has surrounded the birds and focused on two main questions. The first of these is whether the ratites are derived from a single ancestral stock (monophyletic), or whether they are polyphyletic, representing separate evolutionary lines from various groups of birds that have become flightless independently and have come to look alike superficially through convergent evolution. The second perplexing question is whether the ratites represent an ancient group from an early avian evolutionary venture, or are more recently evolved forms that have become highly specialized. Huxley attempted to answer these questions largely on the basis of evidence from the palatal bones. He defined the ratites by their curious palaeognathous palate, which he considered primitive in birds and which many later workers have thought is different from the palate of all other living birds; he thus placed the structure in the center of most subsequent systematic discussions. Nonethe-

The largest living bird, the ostrich *Struthio camelus* (Struthioniformes). Males may reach a height of 8 feet and a weight in excess of 300 pounds. Like the South American rheas, ostriches have unusually long wings and long wing and tail plumes, all used in courtship dances. (Drawing by Yvonne Lee.)

less, other features have been used to argue for or against the antiquity and/or unity of the group, including feather types, pelvic structure, the horny sheath of the bill tip, and the sutures of the skull. The fossil record has contributed little to the discussion, except possibly in the case of the ostrich.

The fossil record of the true ostrich (*Struthio*) begins in the early Pliocene of Eurasia with only one known species, but numerous fossils are known through the late Pleistocene, showing a number of species widespread over the Old World, from southern Russia, Mongolia, China, and India across Europe, as well as in Africa. Presently confined to southern Africa, ostriches until very recently occupied North Africa as well. The last reported Arabian ostrich was killed and eaten during World War II by Saudi Arabian tribesmen. Like most other ratites, ostriches usually roam in small bands of from 10 to 50 birds and eat a variety of foods, including fruits and seeds, other plant matter, insects, and small animals. Although they swim well, ostriches are particularly known for their running speed, and claims of 60 miles per hour have been made.

Joel Cracraft (1974) has recently proposed that African ostriches and South American rheas had a common ancestor that walked across the ancient southern continent of Gondwanaland before it split into South America and Africa some time during the late Cretaceous. But where are the fossils? Ostrich bones are distinctive and as large and heavy as those of many of the large mammalian herbivores; if present,

Map of the world during most of the Cretaceous Period, before the two major continents, Laurasia and Gondwanaland, split into North America and Eurasia, and South America and Africa, respectively, some time in the late Cretaceous.

their fossils would be likely to be found, often in quantity, owing to the birds' gregarious habits. If Cracraft's hypothesis is correct, why do we have no ostrich fossils even from the early Pliocene of Africa? There is an alternative hypothesis: that the ancestor of the ostrich was present in Eurasia as far back as the Eocene, and that the ostrich evolved in Eurasia and only later, in the Pleistocene, became confined to Africa. Let us explore this idea further.

All living birds except the ostrich have three or four toes. The ostrich has only two toes, and therefore only two trochleae, bony structures for the toe articulation, on the end of the tarsometatarsus. This is a running adaptation that converges on similar trends toward reduction in the number of digits in several mammalian lines, especially the horses. Because of this adaptation fossils of the tarsometatarsus belonging to *Struthio* are recognizable at a glance.

A fossil family of gruiform birds that first appeared in the Oligocene of Asia, the Ergilornithidae, shows adaptations of the tarsometatarsus that lead toward the reduction of the toes seen in *Struthio,* and the ergilornithids thus, as Pierce Brodkorb first suggested (1967), provide important clues to the ancestry of ostriches. These ancient gruiform fossils have recently been studied extensively by E. N. Kurochkin (1976) of the Academy of Sciences in Moscow. *Proergilornis minor,* from the early Oligocene of Inner Mongolia, shows the tarsometatarsus with the inner trochlea reduced to a mere stub of bone, indicating a trend toward more cursorial habits than those possessed by its probable ancestor, *Eogrus,* known from the late Eocene of Mongolia. In addition, *Ergilornis rapidus,* also from the early or middle Oligocene of Inner Mongolia, has a tarsometatarsus in which the inner trochlea is largely absent, with only a faint sign of a stub; and the bone is, except for its much smaller size, morphologically similar to the tarsometatarsus of the living ostrich. The continued reduction in the size of the inner trochlea indicates an accelerating trend toward a gracile, cursorial animal. Another fossil of great interest here is *Urmiornis maraghanus,* from the late Miocene to early Pliocene of western Asia. *Urmiornis* was contemporaneous with and probably coexisted with the Pliocene ostrich, and like it, completely lacked the inner trochlea, having attained a degree of cursorial adaptation seen only in the living ostrich.

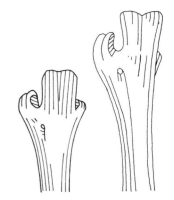

The distal ends of left tarsometatarsi of (left) *Proergilornis,* showing the beginnings of reduction of the inner trochlea, and therefore the inner toe, and (right) *Struthio,* where the inner trochlea is reduced to a mere stub and the inner toe is completely lost. (Drawings by Sigrid K. James.)

The expansive open plains of Mongolia and western Asia seem a logical place to expect the evolution of a fast, cursorial bird such as the ostrich. And the fact that no ostrich fossils older than Pliocene age have been found there, but that ergilornithid fossils occur in this area back to the Oligocene, lends strong support to the idea that ostriches are descended from these ancient gruiforms. Indeed, were it not for the presence of the paleognathous palate in the living ostrich and its absence in the living gruiforms, the derivation of *Struthio* from ergilornithids might well be considered among the best documented lineages in avian paleontology. Possibly the ergilornithids are not ancestral to the ostrich, but are a convergent group present in the appropriate region and at the appropriate geologic time for an ancestral ostrich, but if so, the coincidence is extraordinary.

Another fossil from Mongolia has been proposed as a relative of the ostriches and allies, the late Cretaceous fossil *Gobipteryx* (Elzanowski, 1976), but as Pierce Brodkorb has pointed out, "Neither the specimen . . . nor the published illustrations, are convincingly avian" (1976, p. 67). So, *Gobipteryx* certainly cannot be used as evidence of ratite unity, and cannot aid in resolving the fundamental questions of ratite systematics.

The fossil record of ratites other than the ostrich provides almost no information about ancestry. The rheas (Rheiformes), sometimes called South American ostriches, have left fossils as far back as the Eocene of Argentina, but they tell nothing of evolutionary relationships. The common rhea (*Rhea americana*) once occurred in great flocks across the Brazilian and Argentine pampas; the smaller and still common Darwin's rhea (*Pterocnemia pennata*) occurs in the eastern foothills of the Andes from Peru and Bolivia to the southern tip of South America. Small flocks of rheas, often in company with tinamous and guanocos, roam the open grasslands in search of a variety of vegetable matter, insects, and other small animals. Considerably smaller than the African ostriches, rheas stand 4 to 5 feet tall and weigh about 50 pounds. Still, they are the largest birds in the New World.

The kiwis (order Apterygiformes, family Apterygidae) of New Zealand are represented by three living species, with two more known from the Pleistocene. Named by the native Maoris for their piercing cries, these strange birds live a nocturnal existence in the thick, swampy

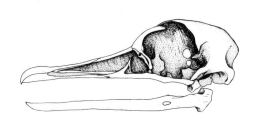

The common rhea (*Rhea americana*),
left; lateral view of its skull, right.
(Drawings by Yvonne Lee.)

tree-fern forests of New Zealand and spend their days in a burrow.
Approximately the size of chickens, they are the smallest of the ratites.
Their wings are truly vestigial, and the 2-inch structures that bear
claws at the tips are completely hidden by their coarse plumage. Both
wing and tail plumes have been lost. A unique feature of the kiwis is
the placement of the nostrils at the very tip of the bill, an adaptation
for locating grubs and worms in the thick humus of the forest floor.
Kiwis nest in underground burrows and lay, relative to body size, the
largest egg (approximately 7 inches long) of any bird. Thought by
some to be most closely related to the giant moas, kiwis are so mani-
festly different morphologically that this seems highly unlikely.

The cassowaries (Casuariiformes, Casuariidae), like the kiwis
known as fossils only from the Pleistocene, share with them the forest
of New Guinea, but are also native to adjacent islands and to northern Australia. Their habitat has favored the adaptation of a casque, or
bony forehead helmet, used to deflect obstructions as they maneuver through dense rain forests. They are also strong swimmers, well
adapted to crossing jungle rivers. They lack tail feathers, have very rudimentary clawed wings only a few inches long, yet have three to five
long wiry quills that are easily seen from the side and tell of their derivation from flying predecessors. Cassowaries are known for their pug-
nacity, and have often killed humans. They attack by leaping at their
enemy feet first, slashing with their powerful, sharp claws. Somewhat
nocturnal, they eat mainly berries and fruits, though they may also
consume small plants and animals.

Skull of the kiwi *Apteryx oweni*, below; the South Island kiwi (*Apteryx australis*), right. (Skull from Simonetta, 1960; kiwi drawing by Yvonne Lee.)

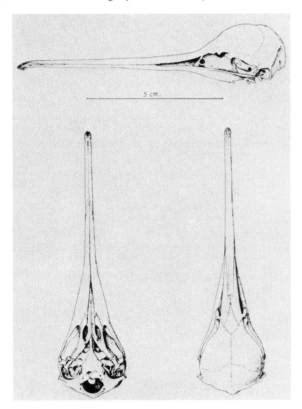

The Australian cassowary (*Casuarius casuarius*), left; its skull, right. (Cassowary drawing by Yvonne Lee; skull from Simonetta, 1960.)

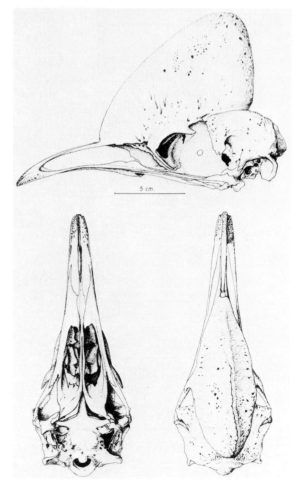

The common emu (*Dromaius novaehol-landiae*). (Drawing by Yvonne Lee.)

Emus (Casuariiformes, Dromaiidae) are closely related to the cassowaries, and like their cousins they swim well, lack tail plumes, and have very rudimentary wing bones with claws at the tips. Now confined to Australia, they were much more diversified during the Pleistocene, when there were several species, and even in modern times three species have vanished from Tasmania and two other smaller islands off the southern coast of Australia. Among the ratites, emus are exceeded in size only by the ostrich, and stand 5 to 6 feet tall and weigh up to 120 pounds. Like the other large ratites, emus live primarily on plant food, but they also eat insects and small animals.

Reconstruction of a typical member of the Dromornithidae, a now extinct family of large terrestrial birds that lived in Australia and are represented by a variety of fossil species extending back to the Miocene. Dromornithids included both highly cursorial and nearly graviportal species. One giant from the late Miocene of the Northern Territory rivaled or possibly exceeded the largest known elephantbird (*Aepyornis*) in size. It is possible that, like phorusrhacids, dromornithids were carnivores, but until fossil skulls of these birds are discovered, we cannot be sure whether they were carnivorous or herbivorous. (Adapted from Rich, 1979.)

The tinamous (Tinamiformes, Tinamidae) are known from the early Pliocene and Pleistocene of Argentina, and approximately 40 modern species range from southern Mexico to Patagonia, inhabiting regions as diverse as the deepest Amazonian jungles, the grassy slopes of the Andean plateaus, and mountainous zones up to 14,000 feet. Tinamous forage entirely on the ground and run rapidly, though they can fly strongly for up to 100 yards when alarmed. Their enigma lies in the fact that they possess the palaeognathous palate seen in all the other ratites—sometimes called true ratites—yet unlike them, tinamous have a keeled sternum. Some consider the tinamous a close ally of the rheas and perhaps near the ancestry of the ratites. Others doubt any ratite relationship at all, and consider the tinamous closely allied to the Galliformes, holding that tinamous have merely retained the palaeognathous palate or have reacquired it through arrested development. It must be said that, aside from the palate, the tinamou skeleton is similar to the galliform skeleton, but both are relatively simple.

The great tinamou (*Tinamus major*). (Drawing by Yvonne Lee.)

Huxley envisioned the ratites, or struthious birds (from *Struthio*, the generic name of the ostrich), as ancient relics of a once great evolutionary radiation: "Though comparatively few genera and species of this order now exist, they differ from one another very considerably, and have a wide distribution, from Africa and Arabia over many of the islands of Malaysia and Polynesia to Australia and South America. Hence, in all probability, the existing Ratitae are but the waifs and strays of what was once a very large and important group" (1867, p. 419). Huxley had proposed to divide the class Aves into three orders: the Saururae, to be represented only by the fossil *Archaeopteryx*; the Ratitae, which comprised the large flightless birds and the kiwi; and the Carinatae, to accommodate all other birds. He was perplexed by the tinamous, which did not fit neatly into either the Ratitae or the Carinatae. Tinamous did possess the palaeognathous palate that Huxley used to group the ratites, but they had the sternum typical of the Carinatae. So, Huxley begins his section on the order Carinatae by stating that it embraces all existing birds except the Ratitae, and then points out that the tinamous are unique among the Carinates in having a completely struthious palate.

Ever since Huxley's time, ornithologists have argued over whether the palaeognathous palate is distinguishable from the neognathous palate, a term used to designate the palates of all living birds except the ratites, and if so what the difference implies for evolutionary relationships. In 1948 Sam McDowell, now of Rutgers University, considered the palaeognathous palate of ratites to be so variable as to defy definition. He recognized four types of palaeognathous palates (with a possible fifth type reserved for the imperfectly preserved elephantbirds). These included the tinamiform type, for rheas and tinamous; the casuariiform type, for cassowaries and emus; the struthioniform type, for the ostrich; and the apterygiform type, for the kiwi.

The palaeognathous palate of the cassowary (above) and the rhea (below).
The prevomers are large and extend
back to articulate with the palatines (at
their posterior ends) and the ptery-
goids, thus separating both from the
parasphenoid rostrum. Large basipterygoid processes are, perhaps, the most
diagnostic feature, but these are also
found in cathartid vultures, some
cranes, and other birds. Some authorities consider that the palaeognathous
palate is not truly definable. (Drawing
by Yvonne Lee.)

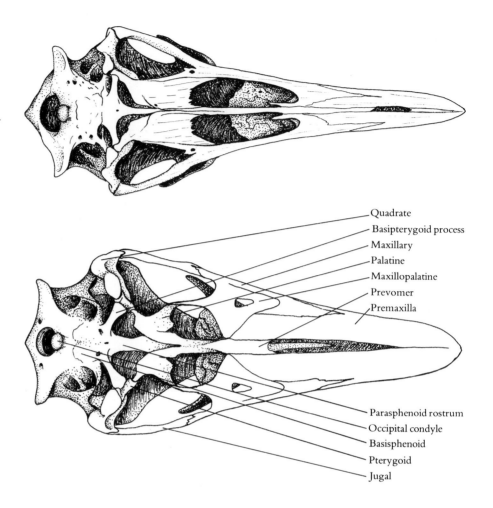

Quadrate
Basipterygoid process
Maxillary
Palatine
Maxillopalatine
Prevomer
Premaxilla

Parasphenoid rostrum
Occipital condyle
Basisphenoid
Pterygoid
Jugal

Obviously, McDowell did not think that the palate could be used as
evidence for a monophyletic ratite assemblage, and in fact, he felt that
the ratite palate could be the result of arrested development because
other features of the ratite skull, such as sutures, are neotenic.

Walter Bock, who does consider the palate definable, maintained
in 1963 that it indicated a common origin of all ratites and tinamous,
but was not primitive in living birds. Stating that the palaeognathous
palate was derived from the neognathous palate, he concluded that
"the ratites do not appear to be primitive among birds . . . nor do
they have to be any older than other typical avian orders" (1963, p.
53). And Gavin de Beer, tackling the palate problem, concluded that
"the palate of the ratites is not primitive but neotenous, and represents
an early stage through which the palate of many Carinates passes during the development period" (1956, p. 5).

Recently, Philip Gingerich (1973, 1976) has demonstrated that the
palaeognathous palate was present even in *Hesperornis,* pointing out
also that the criteria for the palaeognathous palate are met by several
dinosaurs for which the palate is known, including *Tyrannosaurus:*
"The presence of a palaeognathous palate in Mesozoic theropods, 'the
sister group of birds,' together with the palaeognathous palate of the

Cretaceous bird *Hesperornis,* should leave little doubt that the palatal conformation is truly primitive in birds." "Evidence that ratites are strictly monophyletic remains to be discovered" (1976, pp. 31, 32).

But whether or not the palaeognathous palate is primitive among birds is quite separate from the issue of whether or not the ratites themselves are derived from a single ancestor or are a polyphyletic group, inasmuch as the palate could well have arisen at various times through neoteny even if primitive.

Even in Huxley's own era, the palaeognathous palate was being called into question as a panacea for avian systematics. In 1896 Alfred Newton was inclined to view use of the palate with great skepticism:

> The present writer is inclined to think that the characters drawn thence owe more of their worth to the extraordinary perspicuity with which they were presented by Huxley than to their own intrinsic value, and that if the same power had been employed to elucidate in the same way other parts of the skeleton—say the bones of the sternal apparatus or even the pelvic girdle—either set could have been made to appear quite as instructive and perhaps more so. Adventitious value would therefore seem to have been acquired by the bones of the palate through the fact that so great a master of the art of exposition selected them as fitting examples upon which to exercise his skill.   (1896, p. 84)

Another feature used in the attempt to ally the ratites, including the volant tinamous, is a peculiar conformation of the horny sheath, or ramphotheca, of the bill tip, which is segmented rather than a single piece, as in most birds. This character was documented by Kenneth Parkes and George Clark (1966), who argued that all ratites are related. But this feature is present also in certain pelecaniform birds, petrels, and shearwaters (Procellariiformes), and may well be neotenic rather than primitive.

The diversity of morphology shown by the ratite pelvis is another feature arguing against the unity of the group. At the very least, the fast, cursorial ostriches, rheas, and emus should look quite similar in pelvic architecture, but they do not. Ratites also show a great diversity of feather types, although all have feathers more or less uniformly distributed over the body. In cassowaries, emus, and moas, the aftershaft is similar to the main feather in both size and structure, while in the kiwi, as in the ostrich and rhea, the aftershaft is absent. Only tinamous have well-defined and restricted rows of feather growth, or pterylae, and, as A. C. Chandler noted, they "differ from all other birds in having plumules present between the contour feathers while absent in the apteria. The aftershaft is rudimentary or absent in some genera but large and well developed . . . in other genera" (1916, p. 345). After studying the embryology of the nerves and the cranial bones of the ostrich, M. Webb concluded that the ratites are not primitive but rather are "a neotenic offshoot of some ancestral bird or birds" (1957, p. 145).

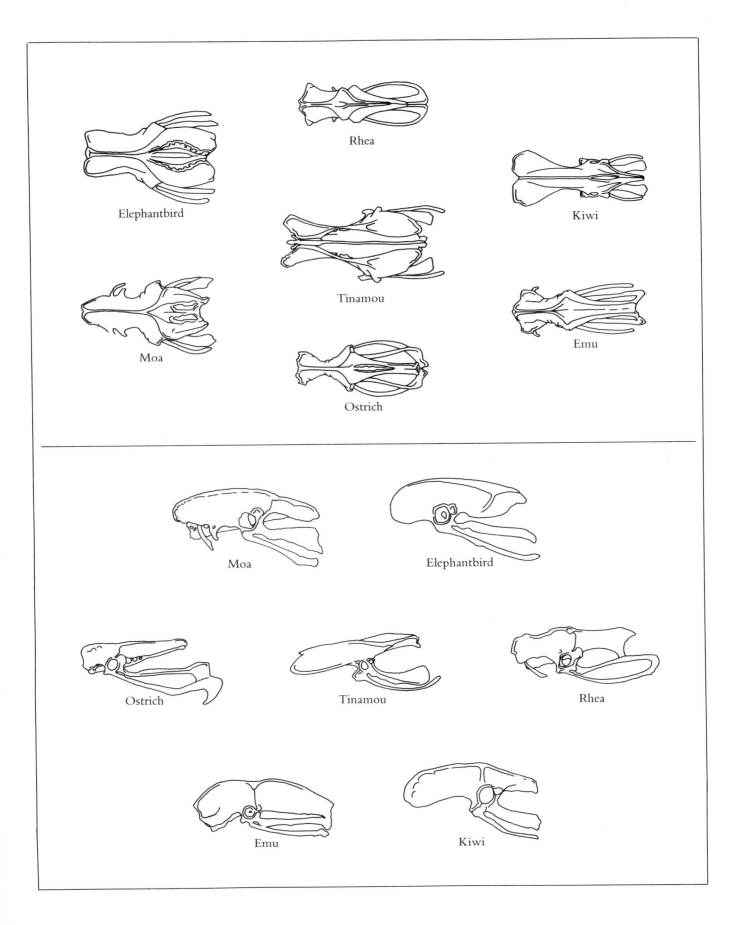

Elephantbird

Rhea

Kiwi

Tinamou

Moa

Emu

Ostrich

Moa

Elephantbird

Ostrich

Tinamou

Rhea

Emu

Kiwi

It may be that the ratites are a paraphyletic group derived from one order of birds, but from different families within the order. This ancestry could perhaps best account for the differences seen in their neotenic forms. If this were the case, the Gruiformes would be the best candidates for some of the various forebears, because, as we have seen, they gave rise in early Tertiary times to several large flightless or nearly flightless forms, such as the diatrymas and phorusrhacids. That these birds did not have palaeognathous palates is no doubt due to strong selection molding their entire feeding apparatus for carnivory. The palaeognathous condition seen in ratites may well be suited only for omnivory and herbivory.

The antiquity of the ratites has also been argued on the basis of the similarity between the hand of the ostrich and the hand of small dinosaurs such as *Ornitholestes* and *Struthiomimus*. However, rudimentary claws or spurs are found in great variety of living birds, ranging from hawks to ducks and rails, and the dinosaurian scapulocoracoid is strictly a neotenic character associated with flightlessness. As we have seen, primitive features in organisms appear earlier in ontogeny than the more specialized. Thus it is not unreasonable to expect numerous primitive characteristics to appear through arrested development in ratites, especially if they are, indeed, "big chicks."

In a series of papers published in 1928b, 1935, and 1944, Percy Lowe proposed that the ratites and the small coelurosaurian dinosaurs, such as *Struthiomimus,* actually did have one common ancestor. Thus, according to Lowe, the ratites were derived from creatures that had never acquired the power of flight. However, although the question has been raised time and time again during the past century, the ratites, like all other flightless birds, clearly have been derived from flying predecessors. We need only look at the vestigial flight quills on the wing of the cassowary to put the question to rest. In addition, the ratites possess the same type of cerebellum found in flying birds, a feature evolved for flight; and the skeleton of the ratite wing is built on the same general plan as that of flying birds, with the fusion of several carpal elements to form a "flight" carpometacarpus. The ratite tail vertebrae are fused to form the uniquely avian pygostyle, a feature also evolved as a flight mechanism. In the rhea the feathers on the first digit are so arranged that they still form the alula, or mid-wing slot, clearly a carinate adaptation that maintains a slip stream in flight.

Dorsal views (above) and lateral views (below) of the pelvises of various true ratites and of a tinamou. Note in the lateral views the large open region, the ilioischiatic fenestra, that characterizes all ratites, but that is also found in the Cretaceous birds *Hesperornis* and *Ichthyornis* and in the embryos of modern birds. Although certainly a neotenic character, it has been used by some to argue that the ratites are related to one another. The enormous diversity in pelvic form is far greater than we would expect if these birds were closely related. Note especially the great difference among the forms adapted for cursorial locomotion—the ostrich, rhea, and emu—which we would expect to look similar if they were related. (Drawings by Sigrid K. James.)

Birds of Prey

7

The birds of prey consist of two groups, the order Falconiformes, including the familiar falcons, hawks, eagles, vultures, and ospreys, as well as the odd secretarybirds, and the order Strigiformes, composed of the owls. Unlike most other birds, these raptorial forms are highly modified in the beak and claws for the seizing of prey.

The order Falconiformes comprises a variety of families thought to be united by certain raptorial adaptations, such as the sharply hooked beak with a soft mass called a cere across its top, through which the nostrils pass, and powerful feet with long claws and an opposable hind toe. Hawks and their allies occur everywhere in the world except Antarctica. Very strong-winged, powerful fliers, many of them are also remarkable soarers, and they all feed almost entirely on animal food, live or dead. They lay a relatively small number of eggs and thus have a low reproductive rate. Unlike the nocturnal owls, falconiforms are primarily diurnal, doing most of their hunting during the daytime.

The fossil record tells us almost nothing about the evolution of raptorial birds. The oldest fossils described as owls have been assigned to a distinctive family, the Bradycnemidae, from the late Cretaceous of England (Harrison and Walker, 1975), but these fossils, along with two other Cretaceous genera, *Wyleyia* (Harrison and Walker, 1973) and *Caenagnathus* (Cracraft, 1971), are in reality small dinosaurs. The oldest reliable record of owls dates back to the Paleocene form *Ogygoptynx* (Rich and Bohaska, 1976), but gives no information on origins or relationships. Fossil hawks go back to the late Eocene or early Oligocene of France in the Old World, and in the New World they are known from the early Oligocene of South America and the middle Oligocene of North America, but they indicate no phylogenetic connections. The order Falconiformes may be polyphyletic, derived from multiple origins (Jollie, 1976), and the relationships between the various families of the Falconiformes are still largely unknown, as are the relationships of the order to other avian groups. Although the hawks were once classified with the owls, it has now become usual to regard owls and hawks as two groups that have become structurally similar in their raptorial adaptations through convergent evolution. Whether

The secretarybird (*Sagittarius serpentarius*). Now confined to East and Central Africa, secretarybirds apparently were once widespread in the Eurasian region and are known from the late Oligocene or early Miocene of France. Secretarybirds seldom take to the air; they systematically walk back and forth across grassy savannahs in pursuit of reptiles, but do not actually run down their prey. When they encounter a reptile, they pound it to death with their feet. (From Van Tyne and Berger, 1976; drawing by George Miksch Sutton.)

The diurnal birds of prey, Falconiformes, represented on the left by the Swainson's hawk (*Buteo swainsoni*), are of unknown origin. Although they were once thought to be related to the nocturnal owls (Strigiformes), represented on the right by the spectacled owl (*Pulsatrix perspicillata*), there is apparently no connection between the two groups. (Drawings by Yvonne Lee.)

or not this is true is still an open question. Nor should the traditional placement of the Falconiformes next to the Galliformes be construed as having any phylogenetic implications; there is little if any evidence to connect falconiform and gallinaceous birds. Moreover, the conventional placement of the Falconiformes after the ducks, geese, and swans (Anseriformes) is unreasonable; ducks, as we saw in Chapter 5, are clearly derived from ancient shorebird stock. Indeed, the question of the relationships of the various families of diurnal raptors to one another and to other avian orders remains one of the major challenges of avian systematics.

Perhaps the most puzzling groups are the vultures. Large, repugnant, bare-headed carrion-eaters, the vultures really comprise two distinct families having little to do with each other in an evolutionary sense. There are the New World vultures (family Cathartidae), of unknown ancestry but thought by some to be allied with the storks, and the Old World vultures, which share the large family Accipitridae (205 species) with a variety of forms ranging from hawks and eagles to the small kites.

Like the storks, New World vultures cool themselves by dumping their urinary liquids onto their hind legs, a process called urohidrosis that accounts for the characteristic buildup of whitish uric acid on their legs. With their powerful wings, New World vultures are excellent soarers, perhaps the world's best. There are seven living species, including the nearly extinct California condor and the Andean condor, very large birds weighing up to 25 pounds and having a wing span of almost 10 feet. The other five are the king vulture, which ranges from southern Mexico to Argentina; the smaller, more familiar black and turkey vultures; and two yellow-headed forms. All of them

Convergent evolution has given a similar appearance to the New World vultures, represented on the left by the king vulture (*Sarcoramphus papa*), and the Old World vultures, represented on the right by the Indian white-backed vulture (*Gyps bengalensis*). The two groups are certainly not closely related. (Drawings by Yvonne Lee.)

The Andean condor (*Vultur gryphus*), one of the largest living flying birds. (Photo by the author.)

The African white-backed vulture (*Gyps africanus*) at an abandoned lion's kill of a young Cape buffalo on the Loita Plains of Kenya. Note the marabou stork in the foreground of the lower picture at far right, its legs white from excretion of uric acid. A whitened stork's leg can also be seen above the vulture's beak in the closeup at near right. (Photos by the author.)

have long front toes with a slight web at their base, not adapted for grasping, and elevated hind toes. They have a longitudinal nasal opening, but the absence of a voice box prevents them from making any sound except a hissing noise.

The Old World vultures, while they share the characteristic bare head associated with carrion-eating, differ from New World vultures in possessing strongly hooked feet, rounded nasal openings, and a voice box. Derived from eaglelike ancestors, the Old World vultures constitute the distinctive subfamily Aegypiinae. In size, they range from the gigantic griffons and eared vultures to the diminutive Egyptian vulture (*Neophron percnopterus*), which today ranges throughout Africa and eastward through Arabia to India, feeding indiscriminately on any kind of garbage or carrion.

Presently confined to Africa and Asia, the Old World vultures are, surprisingly, represented in the Tertiary and Quaternary fossil record of North America. In 1916, Loye Miller described a fossil specimen of *Neophrontops americanus,* an Old World vulture closely related to the modern Egyptian vulture, along with another Old World vulture, *Neogyps errans,* from the Pleistocene Rancho La Brea tarpits in the distinctively New World setting of southern California. Miller later admitted that "announcement was withheld for two years because of the wide geographic separation from other members of the Old World vulture group" (Miller and Demay, 1942, p. 95). Since Miller's initial discovery, many other Old World fossils, representing three diverse genera, have been discovered from the early Miocene (*Palaeoborus*), the Pliocene, and the Pleistocene of North America. But since Old World vultures also occur as fossils back to the early Miocene of the Old World (*Palaeohierax*), the fossil record provides little evidence of their place of origin.

The New World vultures, now confined to the Western Hemisphere, have left a variety of fossil remains in Europe. The fossil cathartids found in the Old World are first represented by *Eocathartes,* known from two species from the middle Eocene of Germany. One species is based only on a foot bone, the other on a badly flattened skeleton in which most of the bones are crushed or greatly damaged. The genera *Plesiocathartes* and *Diatropornis,* known from upper Eocene to middle Oligocene deposits in France, are both relatively small New World vultures, one species being only about half as large as that of the living North American turkey vulture. The only other Old World genus, *Amphiserpentarius,* may have occurred as late as the early Miocene of France, but there is no evidence of any cathartids in the Old World past the early Miocene.

The oldest fossil ever considered to be a New World vulture, a species firmly implanted in most ornithology textbooks, is the "running vulture" described in 1944 as *Neocathartes grallator* by Alexander Wetmore, who placed it in its own family, the Neocathartidae. Known from the late Eocene of Wyoming, this fossil was for some time thought to be a long-legged, cursorial cathartid with reduced wings. But *Neocathartes,* currently under study by Storrs Olson, clearly belongs to an unrelated order of birds. It may have been this fossil, superficially reminiscent of storks, that led some to postulate a relationship between storks and cathartids. The earliest forms now assigned to the Cathartidae in the New World are *Palaeogyps* and *Phasmagyps,* from the early Oligocene of Colorado. Most biogeographers have thought that the New World vultures originated in the New World because of their current distribution, but the fossil record, showing nearly coeval forms from both the New and Old Worlds, makes it clear that no decision can be made.

The fossil Old World vultures known from the New World. (From Feduccia, 1974a; information primarily from Brodkorb, 1964.)

Species	Range	Age
Palaeoborus rosatus A. H. Miller & Compton	South Dakota	Early Miocene
Palaeoborus howardae Wetmore	Nebraska	Middle Miocene
Palaeoborus umbrosus (Cope)	New Mexico	Early Pliocene
Neophrontops vetustus Wetmore	Nebraska	Middle Miocene
Neophrontops dakotensis Compton	South Dakota, Oregon	Early and middle Pliocene
Neophrontops slaughteri Feduccia	Idaho	Late Pliocene
Neophrontops vallecitoensis Howard	California	Middle Pleistocene
Neophrontops americanus L. Miller	California, New Mexico, Mexico	Late Pleistocene
Neogyps errans L. Miller	California, Nevada, Mexico, Colorado	Late Pleistocene

Temporal ranges of the Cathartidae. The ranges of *Plesiocathartes, Diatropornis,* and *Amphiserpentarius* are estimated from the available evidence. (Adapted from Cracraft and Rich, 1972.)

	OLD WORLD	NEW WORLD
RECENT		*Cathartes* *Gymnogyps* *Breagyps* *Coragyps*
PLEISTOCENE		
PLIOCENE		*Pliogyps* *Vultur* *Sarcoramphus*
MIOCENE		
OLIGOCENE	*Amphiserpentarius*	*Phasmagyps* *Palaeogyps*
EOCENE	*Plesiocathartes* *Diatropornis* *Eocathartes*	

The La Brea condor (*Breagyps clarki*).
(Courtesy of D. P. Whistler and the
Natural History Museum of Los Angeles County.)

Aside from the two genera of North American cathartids from the early Oligocene, there is a hiatus in the fossil record until Pliocene time, when New World vultures again appear in the form of *Sarcoramphus,* ancestral to the king vulture, and *Vultur,* ancestral to the Andean condor. Also known from the Pliocene is *Pliogyps,* a form distantly related to living cathartids. Why New World vultures should not have persisted in Europe after early Miocene time is simply not understood. Possibly they disappeared because they could not compete with the Old World vultures, which were then on the ascent.

During the Pleistocene of North America, the cathartids, along with the Old World vultures, multiplied in almost incredible numbers. The ancestor of the black vulture, *Coragyps,* and the ancestor of the turkey vulture, *Cathartes,* arose in this period, along with a wide vari-

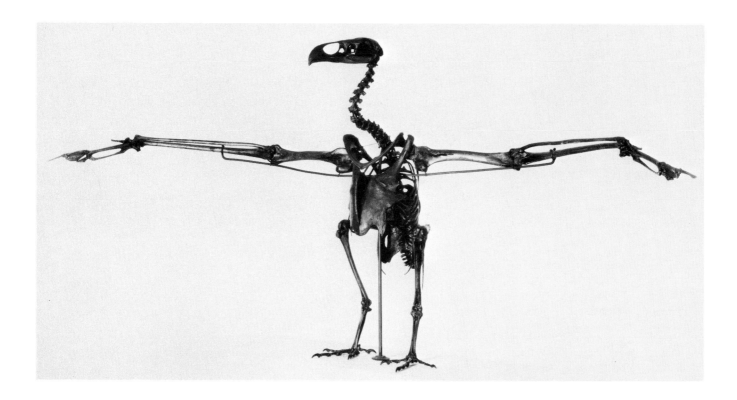

ety of other forms, including the now extinct La Brea condor (*Brea-gyps clarki*) and the once widespread California condor (*Gymnogyps*). Perhaps the most remarkable of the Ice Age vulturine birds found in the New World were the teratorns (subfamily Teratornithinae), a group similar to but possibly not related to cathartids. The very common *Teratornis merriami* had a wing span of 11 to 12 feet, and *Teratornis incredibilis,* known from Pleistocene deposits in Nevada and California, had a wing span that may have approached 17 feet. But the real giant was an Argentine fossil recently described by Kenneth Campbell and Eduardo Tonni (1980). This huge form, nearly twice the size of *Teratornis merriami,* stood 5 feet tall and had a wing span of about 24 feet; it is the largest flying bird known to science. Teratorns were widely distributed, and as fossils are known from Florida, Mexico, California, and Argentina.

Much of our knowledge of the Ice Age avifauna comes from fossils preserved in asphalt deposits such as the Rancho La Brea tarpits near Los Angeles. Lying under Pleistocene waterholes, these tarry sediments often seeped to the surface, trapping the mammals and birds that gathered there to drink. Twelve orders of birds comprising 125 species are represented at La Brea. Over half of these are falconiforms, probably present in such great numbers because as carrion-eaters they flocked to waterholes to feed on dead or moribund prey trapped in the mire. The large vulturine population was easily sustained by the immense numbers of mammals that thrived in the North American

The Merriam teratorn (*Teratornis merriami*), from the Pleistocene of Rancho La Brea, California, with a wing span of 11 to 12 feet. (Courtesy of D. P. Whistler and the Natural History Museum of Los Angeles County.)

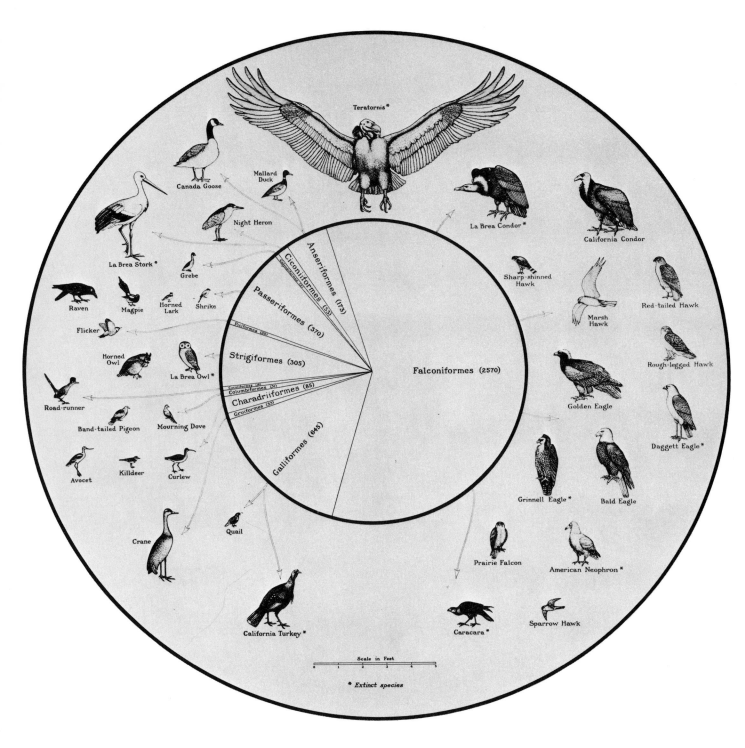

The diversity of birds in the Rancho La Brea fauna. The numbers refer to the fossils found. (Courtesy of D. P. Whistler and the Natural History Museum of Los Angeles County.)

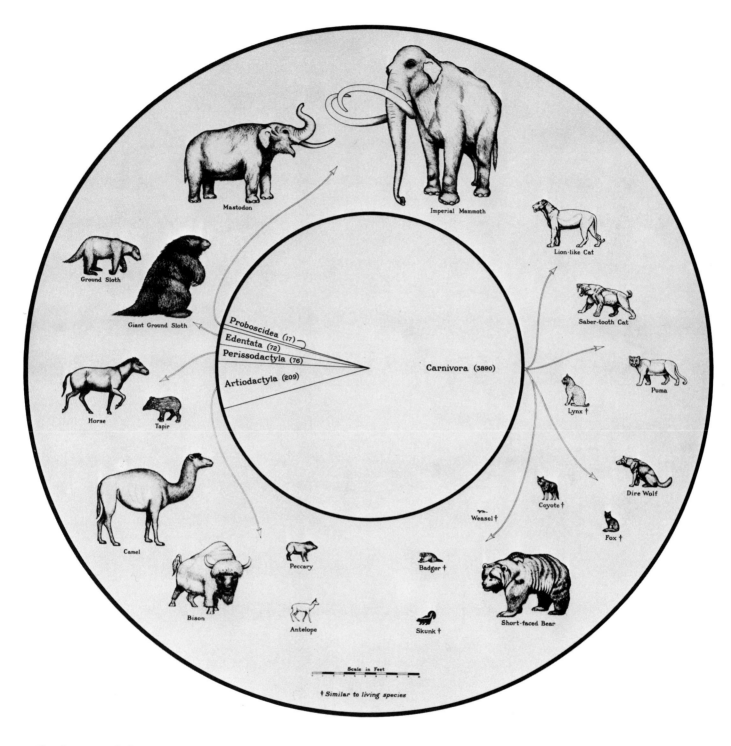

The diversity of Pleistocene mammals recovered from the Rancho La Brea tarpits, not including insectivores, bats, rodents, and rabbits. The numbers refer to the fossils found. (Courtesy of D. P. Whistler and the Natural History Museum of Los Angeles County.)

Reconstruction of a Pleistocene water-hole at Rancho La Brea approximately 100,000 years ago. The dire wolf (*Canis dirus*) on the left, and the saber-toothed tiger (*Smilodon*), on the right, came to prey on other animals and were at times trapped themselves. In the right rear is a group of horses of an extinct species. The large teratorns waited to feed upon the carcasses of mired animals. (Mural by Charles R. Knight; courtesy of the Field Museum of Natural History, Chicago.)

Pleistocene. Carnivores included the saber-toothed tiger, the cheetah, and the lionlike cat. Herbivorous mammals were even more numerous, and included, to mention only a few, two common elephants—the mastodon and larger imperial mammoth—camels, horses, tapirs, giant and smaller ground sloths, bison, peccaries, and antelopes.

By the end of the Pleistocene, most of these large mammals were extinct, and so were the Old World vultures, the teratorns, and most of the New World vultures that fed on them. The cause of this massive extinction has been controversial. Sixty-seven genera of mammals had disappeared by the end of the Ice Age, but nearly half of these died out in the narrow time interval of 12,000 to 8,000 years ago. Paul S. Martin (1973) has developed a theory, usually referred to as the Pleistocene overkill hypothesis, to explain the extinction of mammals during this period. According to Martin, prehistoric hunters, crossing into North America over the Bering land bridge, killed off much of the mammalian fauna, thus exterminating many of the animals that vultures preyed on. But Martin's hypothesis does not account for the simultaneous extinction of at least 10 avian genera (Grayson, 1977) and the disappearance of such small forms as pocket gophers. It appears more likely that the extirpation of so many species was due to a sudden change in climate from the generally mild conditions obtaining through most of the Pleistocene to the harsher climatic extremes that now characterize North America.

Excavation of fossil bones at Rancho La Brea, showing the exposure of bones of Ice Age animals in the asphalt. (Courtesy of D. P. Whistler and the Natural History Museum of Los Angeles County.)

The Rise of Land Birds

8

Birds originated in the trees. *Archaeopteryx,* the first known bird, was arboreal, and there is no reason not to think that the first "modern" birds were similarly adapted. Nor does the paleontological record tell us differently. The first modern waterbirds are from the late Cretaceous, as is the first modern land bird, *Alexornis,* a species described by Pierce Brodkorb (1976) as possibly intermediate between the piciform and coraciiform birds. The real question seems to be whether modern waterbirds came soon after, or much later than, modern arboreal land birds. Convention has placed the arboreal land birds at the apex of the avian classification, and the same conventional practice has led me to end this book with them; but there is really no reason to suppose that this is a logical sequence. The birds that are most highly modified from the ancestral design, and that one would like to place at the end of the avian classification, are actually such specialized groups as the penguins, the loons, or even the ratites. In any case, there are living birds that can, with little question, be considered primitive land birds —the Cuculiformes and their allies—and these, together with certain critical fossils that have recently come to light, permit us to reconstruct a history, albeit hazy, of the rise of land birds.

The coraciiforms, piciforms, and passeriforms and their allies have perhaps presented more problems than any other avian groups in resolving their phylogenetic relationships. These particular groups are extremely similar structurally, and despite over a century of morphological and other studies there have been very few clues, either from structure or from the fossil record, that have aided in our understanding of the evolution of these groups.

Most phylogenetic studies of avian structures have suffered from one major drawback: the inability to establish unequivocally the primitive nature of the particular structure or structures involved. For example, one might tend to think that the Cretaceous toothed birds *Ichthyornis* and *Hesperornis* shared a common ancestor because they both possess very similar teeth. But such a trait cannot be used as evidence for relatedness because it is a *retained* primitive reptilian characteristic. Likewise, the presence of feathers in a grebe and a loon cannot be used as evidence that they shared an immediate common ancestor because

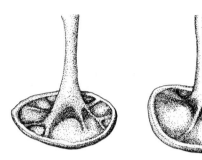

The primitive avian stapes, or columella, of the kiwi, *Apteryx* (left), and of a passerine bird, *Coracina* (right). Here both are drawn to similar size for easy comparison. (From Feduccia, 1977c.)

the ultimate ancestor of all birds had feathers. However, if we can establish that a certain characteristic of various birds is unique and derived—evolved beyond the primitive condition—then we would have strong evidence for evolutionary affinity. Therefore, the first step in any evolutionary study of structural characteristics is to establish whether the trait is primitive or derived, and in most cases in birds this has been an extremely difficult task.

Much new evidence has come to light through studies of the structure of the avian middle-ear ossicle, the stapes, or columella. The avian stapes was one of the last remaining elements of the skeleton to be studied in detail, no doubt because of its minute size (1 to several millimeters), its fragility, and its remote location in the recesses of the middle-ear system. Over the past decade I have examined more than 2,000 specimens, representing nearly all of the living families of birds, and have reported these findings in various journals (see Feduccia, 1975). The columella has provided an exceptional opportunity for phylogenetic analysis because its primitive nature can be established beyond doubt. Unlike the mammalian middle-ear system, in which there are three bony ossicles (the malleus, incus, and stapes) that transmit sound vibrations from the tympanic membrane to the fluids of the inner ear, the avian middle ear, like that of reptiles, has a single stapes that performs the same function. It is a simple structure that consists of a flat footplate that fits into the oval window of the inner ear; its straight bony shaft connects via its ligaments to the tympanic membrane.

The vast majority of living birds possess the primitive condition of the bony stapes that is homologous with the same element in reptiles and represents a retained primitive character. Therefore, where pockets of unique, derived morphologies occur, they must be strong evidence for evolutionary relationships. Fortunately, within several groups of the arboreal land birds we find these unique, derived middle-ear ossicles, and they have aided greatly in our understanding of interrelationships. In addition we can rely on comparisons of other skeletal and muscular features, such as the voice box and the feet.

If we begin our survey of arboreal land birds with the Cuculiformes, considered by many to be among the most primitive of the

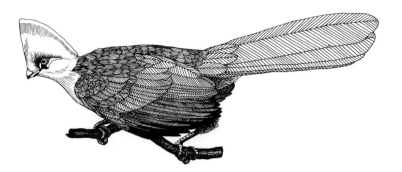

The Knysna touraco (*Tauraco corythaix*) of South Africa, an 18-inch-long forest species. (Drawing by Sigrid K. James, after Austin, 1961.)

group, we find that their stapes also is primitive, and therefore not a useful indicator of affinity. The members of this order are the cuckoos and their distant allies the South American hoatzins (Opisthocomidae) and the African touracos (Musophagidae). Except for the hoatzins, these birds are zygodactyl, having a yoke-toed foot with the outer toe reversed.

The cuckoos themselves, represented by 127 species distributed throughout the tropical and temperate regions of the world, show very complex zoogeographic patterns, no doubt related to the antiquity of the group. Their current success is probably due in part to their perfection of the art of brood parasitism. Most species of cuckoos deposit a single egg in each of several nests of one or more host species. In many cases, these eggs almost perfectly match the color and pattern of the host's eggs; when the young cuckoo hatches it usually ejects its nestmates. Cuckoos are a reasonably tightly knit group morphologically, but there are more than a dozen large terrestrial forms, such as the roadrunners, that show marked structural modification for a ground-dwelling existence. The fossil record of the cuckoos goes back to the early Tertiary, but it is very sparse and the bones tell us nothing of cuculiform affinities.

Most touracos inhabit the deep forests of Africa, although several of the 19 living species are bushland forms. Their food consists mainly of fruit, with some insects as a supplement. Several fossil touracos have been reported from the late Eocene or early Oligocene and the Miocene of France, and show that these birds were once widespread, at least in the Old World.

The South American hoatzin (*Opisthocomus hoazin*), once placed in the order Galliformes, is now generally conceded to belong within or close to the cuculiform complex. Confined to trees along river banks in the Amazon Basin, these colonial birds are primarily leaf-eaters, and have a large crop like that of the galliform birds. Their most distinctive feature is the two-clawed hands of hoatzin chicks that enable them to climb back up to the nest after they have dropped into the water when threatened. These claws are a secondary evolutionary innovation, and not a feature retained from primitive birds, such as *Archaeopteryx*. There is a fossil hoatzin from the Miocene of Colombia, but it offers no information concerning the relationships of this interesting bird. Other fossils referred by some to this group are too fragmentary to be reliably identified as hoatzins.

Altogether, the cuculiform complex appears to be a fairly early offshoot of the line leading to the modern land birds, and probably first appeared in the Cretaceous, although fossils to verify this have yet to be found.

A group thought by some to be related to the cuculiforms are the African mousebirds, or colies. Colies are sufficiently unusual morphologically to rank as a separate order, the Coliiformes, and probably represent another early line that diverged from the mainstream of land bird evolution. Colies have a peculiar foot in which the outer and hind toes are reversible and can be used either forward or backward, so that there may be either two, three, or four toes pointing forward. These colonial birds behave in much the same manner as members of the titmouse family, often clinging upside down while gleaning foliage for insects, though they can feed in almost any position. Now confined to Africa south of the Sahara, the colies were reported from the Miocene of Europe by Peter Ballmann (1969a), and therefore must have been more widespread in the past.

Of unknown origin but probably derived from ancient land birds are the goatsuckers and allies of the order Caprimulgiformes. Active primarily in the evening and at night, these birds are characterized by very small feet and enormous gaping mouths adapted for catching insects. Except for the South American oilbird (Steatornithidae), a cave-dwelling echolocator that eats palm fruits at night, all are primarily insectivorous. The most successful family is the nightjars, the Caprimulgidae, which contains 67 species and has a worldwide distribution. The other three families are the South American potoos (Nyctibiidae), the Australian frogmouths (Podargidae), and the Australian owlet-frogmouths (Aegothelidae). The last two are relict families that resemble the true owls, both in behavior and in external appearance and

The mousebirds, or colies (order Coliiformes), represented here by the bar-breasted coly (*Colius striatus*), are arboreal acrobats, and like the parrots use the bill in climbing. (Drawing by Yvonne Lee.)

structure. The frogmouths have strongly hooked bills, and feed by fluttering down to the ground from a perch to catch beetles, centipedes, caterpillars, and even mice. The owlet-frogmouths, called by Australians moth owls, closely resemble small, long-tailed owls. They feed like the frogmouths, and also seize insects on the wing. Like owls, they sit crossways instead of lengthwise on branches, nest in hollow trees, and hatch young that are covered with down. Perhaps these living relics indicate a link between ancient caprimulgiforms and owls.

Although the origins of caprimulgiform birds remain elusive, there is a possible link, based on certain morphological similarities, between the goatsuckers and the swifts (Apodidae) in the strange crested swifts (Hemiprocnidae) of southeast Asia and adjacent islands. Fossils of both caprimulgiform birds and swifts are known from the Eocene or Oligocene of France, but these bones fail to indicate any evolutionary affinity.

Another group often linked to the swifts is the hummingbirds (Trochilidae), a very successful New World neotropical family of 319 species. Almost certainly of post-Cretaceous origin because of their South American distribution, these small nectar-eating birds are somewhat convergent on the Old World passeriform sunbirds, the Nectariniidae. Hummingbirds have usually been placed with the swifts in a single order, the Apodiformes, but they may not be related to swifts, and it is probably more reasonable to assign them to the separate order Trochiliformes, as some authorities have done. The hummingbirds' true alliance may well be with the passerine birds, with which they share a number of important anatomical characteristics (Sibley and Ahlquist, 1972, pp. 200–205).

The birds generally called "coraciiforms" are a diverse group whose best-known representatives in the Northern Hemisphere are the kingfishers. Classical systematics considered the order Coraciiformes to be comprised of ten distinctive families of brightly colored

One of the eight species of owlet-frogmouths, *Aegotheles insignis*. (From Van Tyne and Berger, 1976; drawing by George Miksch Sutton.)

The crested swift (*Hemiprocne longipennis*), right, provides a possible link between caprimulgiform birds and the swifts; shown to the left is a representative caprimulgiform, the common nighthawk (*Chordeiles minor*). (Drawings by Sigrid K. James; crested swift after Austin, 1961.)

The chimney swift (*Chaetura pelagica*)
and a hummingbird, the racquet-tail
(*Loddigesia mirabilis*). The cosmopolitan
swifts (family Apodidae) and the New
World hummingbirds are thought by
many to be related, but their relationships are unknown. (Drawings by
Yvonne Lee.)

The African lilac-breasted roller (*Cora-
cias caudata*), right. Shown above are
silhouettes of primitive Madagascan
relicts: the cuckoo roller (*Leptosomus*),
center; and the ground rollers *Uratelornis,* left, and *Brachypteracias,* right.
(Drawings by Sigrid K. James; lilac-
breasted roller after Austin, 1961.)

A ground hornbill (*Bucorvus leadbeateri*) stalking the Loita Plains in Kenya. This one eventually caught a snake and flew off. (Photo by the author.)

subtropical and tropical land birds. These forms represent an early attempt at becoming arboreal land birds, and some can now be considered relicts. Coraciiforms arose in the Old World and were the predominant birds of the Oligocene, enjoying dynamic evolution and widespread distribution. Few anatomical characteristics bind these birds together, but they do share rather small feet that have an unusual toe arrangement in which the three anterior toes are joined for part of their length, a condition known as syndactyly. Most coraciiform birds are carnivorous, eating small fish, amphibians and reptiles, small mammals and insects. In addition, they are cavity nesters, digging holes in banks or rotten trees.

Percy Lowe summarized our knowledge of coraciiform evolutionary relationships by saying that "the Coraciiformes have for many years been loaded with a heterogeneous collection of forms which custom has blindly accepted" (1948, p. 572). However, recent studies permit us to distinguish between the ancient relicts and the derived forms.

Two groups of coraciiforms possess the primitive, reptilian form of the middle-ear ossicle, the various rollers and the hornbills. Centered in the Old World tropics are the 17 species of the Coraciidae, or rollers, so named for their aerial acrobatics. They are known from the Eocene or Oligocene of France, but the fossil record tells little other than that there was once a widespread distribution. Even more primitive are two relicts now confined to Madagascar, the ground rollers (Brachypteraciidae) and the cuckoo rollers (Leptosomatidae). Ancient forms resembling these relict groups may well have been ancestral to the passerine birds and, perhaps, the piciform and other land bird groups as well. The hornbills (Bucerotidae) of the Old World tropics are some of the most bizarre of all birds, with their enormous, downcurved bills, often surmounted by a large horny casque. Their food is for the most part fruits and berries, but some may eat insects, small mammals, and snakes. Hornbills are somewhat convergent on the New World tropical toucans of the order Piciformes.

A wood hoopoe, *Phoeniculus* (above), and a hoopoe *Upupa* (below), with the unique anvil stapes possessed by both. (From Feduccia, 1977c; drawing by Yvonne Lee.)

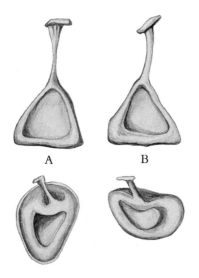

Posterior views (above) and views looking down upon the footplate regions (below) of the stapes of *A*, a typical suboscine passerine bird, and *B*, a typical member of the bee-eater/kingfisher/motmot/tody/trogon assemblage (Alcediniformes). All are drawn to approximately the same size. (From Feduccia, 1977c.)

Another group of coraciiform birds comprises the hoopoes (Upupidae) and wood hoopoes (Phoeniculidae). These birds have often been placed in separate families, as indicated here, and are considered by many to be only very distantly related, if at all. However, their unique, derived, anvil-shaped middle-ear bones tell us differently; that both groups have such a bizarre structure would seem to argue strongly for a close evolutionary relationship. Both are also from the Old World, and wood hoopoes are presently confined to Africa south of the Sahara. Hoopoes extend into Europe, and a large flightless hoopoe, now extinct, existed on the South Atlantic island of St. Helena during Pleistocene time or later (Olson, 1975b). A wood hoopoe is now known from the Miocene of Bavaria; this find, combined with reports of touracos and colies from deposits of similar age in Europe (Ballmann, 1969a, 1969b), indicates that Europe had a much warmer climate then than now, and that the present Ethiopian avifauna—hoopoes, colies, and touracos—was once extensive in its range.

The remaining "coraciiform" families include the bee-eaters (Meropidae), kingfishers (Alcedinidae), motmots (Momotidae), todies (Todidae), and the trogons, which have usually been placed in their own order, the Trogoniformes. This assemblage is a group of derived birds that are clearly united by their peculiar middle-ear ossicles, characterized by a large, bulbous footplate region. These ossicles are somewhat similar to those of the suboscine passerine birds, and this likeness led me at one time to conclude that the two groups might have shared a common ancestor (Feduccia, 1975, 1977c). However, it is

Scanning electron micrographs of three views along the lengths of the bony stapes of: (right) a trogon (*Priotelus temnurus*), (middle) a kingfisher (*Ceryle rudis*), and (left) a suboscine passerine (*Rupicola peruviana*). The SEM's were taken so as to have all to approximately the same scale; they are from approximately ×25 to ×35, and are here reduced ×1/2. (From Feduccia, 1979.)

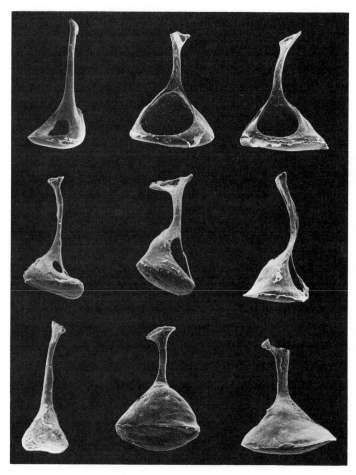

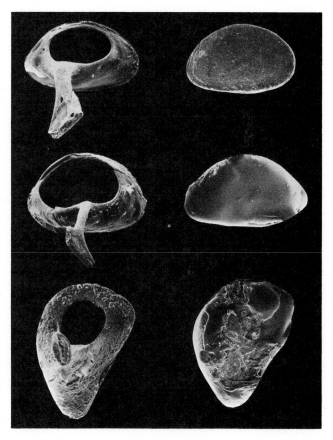

apparent from my more recent studies using the scanning electron microscope that the two types are quite different and clearly distinct from each other. I have suggested (Feduccia, 1977c) that the bee-eater/kingfisher/motmot/tody/trogon assemblage be split off from the other Coraciiformes as the order Alcediniformes, and this category will be used here.

The 24 species of bee-eaters are very colorful, social birds that range throughout the Old World, particularly in tropical regions. They are particularly fond of wasps and bees, and forage by flying out to catch them on the wing. Bee-eaters nest colonially, and like many coraciiforms, dig their burrows in dirt banks.

Scanning electron micrographs of views of the tops (left) and bottoms (right) of the footplates of a trogon (above), kingfisher (middle), and suboscine (below). The species are the same as in the accompanying figure. The SEM's are from ×45 to ×55, and are here reduced ×1/2 (From Feduccia, 1979.)

The nearly cosmopolitan kingfishers appear to be the only birds in the "coraciiform" complex to have become well adapted physiologically to the variable climate of the temperate zone. They are clearly an Old World group that apparently has just recently invaded the New World across the Bering land bridge that connected Eurasia and North America in the late Tertiary. Kingfishers range in size from very small forms about 5 inches in length to the 17-inch-long laughing kookaburra. Although best known for their invasion of the fishing niche, which avoided competition with more advanced land birds, kingfishers are actually quite diverse in feeding habits, ranging from our familiar fishermen to Old World forest kingfishers that never go near water, but hunt for insects and small vertebrates. The kookaburra is quite fond of snakes and even the young of other birds. Like bee-eaters, kingfishers nest in burrows in dirt banks. The worldwide distribution of the kingfisher family is quite deceiving, for of the 82 living species, only 6 (all closely related) occur in the New World, and there is only one European species, a form widespread over the Old World. Fifteen species occur in Africa, and the remaining 60 range from Asia southward to Australia, occurring on Pacific islands as far east as Samoa.

The eight species of motmots are moderate-sized forest birds restricted at present to the neotropics, from Mexico south to northern Argentina. The todies are tiny relatives of the motmots that are survived today by five species restricted to the West Indies, the only family of birds confined to that area. Both todies and motmots nest in burrows and eat insects, though motmots are also known to eat small vertebrates and some fruit. Motmots have long tails with racket tips, and both motmots and todies have broad, flattened bills with serrations along the edges.

Both forms were probably widespread in mid-Tertiary time, but in the late Tertiary a combination of climatic deterioration and competition with more advanced land birds entirely eliminated the tody-motmot assemblage from the Old World regions. The same changes in the New World resulted in the restriction of the range of motmots to Central America; they have spread into South America since the closing of the Panamanian seaway and the opening of the Central American land bridge, now accurately dated at 5.7 million years ago (Raven and Axelrod, 1975). Similar changes no doubt affected the North American todies. A fossil tody, *Palaeotodus emryi,* is known from the Oligocene of Wyoming (Olson, 1976), showing that todies were once widespread in the New World, and are only restricted to the West Indies as relicts. Their ultimate origin, however, is unknown. Motmots appear to be a group of Old World origin, since there is a fossil, *Protornis glarniensis,* from the Oligocene of France that seems to be closely allied with the motmots. The motmots could have crossed over the Bering land bridge, and, with the late Tertiary climatic deteri-

Representatives of the living families of the Alcediniformes, united by their possession of a unique type of middle-ear bone (center). Upper left, the Cuban tody (*Todus multicolor*), family Todidae, a relict group of five species now confined to the West Indies; upper right, the blue-crowned motmot (*Momotus momota*), family Momotidae, of the New World tropics; left center, the European bee-eater (*Merops apias-ter*), family Meropidae, of the Old World; lower left, the belted kingfisher (*Megaceryle alcyon*), family Alcedinidae, nearly worldwide in distribution; and lower right, the collared trogon (*Trogon collaris*), family Trogonidae, now confined as a relict group to the Old and New World tropics, particularly Central America. (Drawing by Melissa Marshall.)

oration and competition from advanced passerines, have become restricted to the Central American region, only recently venturing into South America. Storrs Olson, in discussing *Palaeotodus,* has suggested that "perhaps with material from earlier in the Oligocene it would not be possible to distinguish the two families, the family Todidae having assumed its characteristics since that time" (1976, p. 118). James Bond in 1966 had expressed reservations about the ability of todies to cross even narrow water gaps because of the feeble flight of modern species, but *Palaeotodus* was a larger bird and showed proportions suggestive of greater powers of flight.

Like the motmots and todies, the trogons have spread into South America since the opening of the Central American land bridge. Trogons are well represented in the fossil record of the Old World, going back to the Eocene or Oligocene of France; they probably dispersed into the New World through the Bering land bridge and were forced southward by late Tertiary climatic deterioration. Today they appear only sparsely in South America, occurring mostly in the Central American–West Indian region.

The 34 species of trogons (Trogonidae), the most famous being the Central American quetzal, occur in the tropics of both the Old and New Worlds. Famous for their resplendent iridescent plumage, the trogons are clearly the most divergent structurally of the alcediniform birds. In addition to a feathered tarsus, they have a unique type of yoke-toed foot called heterodactyl, in which the inner, or second, toe is shifted to the rear; in the zygodactyl foot of woodpeckers, cuckoos, and parrots, it is the outer, or fourth, toe that has migrated backward. Trogons feed in flycatcher fashion, eating insects extensively, along with some fruits. Like other alcediniforms, they are cavity nesters, but the nest is usually excavated in rotten wood or a termite nest rather than a dirt bank. The trogons are of great zoogeographic interest because their remains are known from the Eocene or Oligocene and the Miocene of France (*Archaeotrogon* and *Paratrogon*), indicating a much more extensive distribution in the past. The present-day New World species, like the motmots, are primarily Central American in distribution. In Central America and the West Indies there are 16 species placed in 5 genera; in South America, 14 species in 2 genera.

The order Piciformes is best known by the tree-creeping, or scansorial, woodpeckers (family Picidae). However, the order is composed primarily of perching birds, and the characteristic feature of the group is the zygodactyl foot, which originally evolved as a perching foot in the early members of the order, and was later modified for foraging along tree trunks. While the bird hitches up tree trunks, the toes are spread to the side as an aid in climbing.

Dating back well into Eocene time in North America, some 50 million years ago, the order is certainly a primitive one. One extinct

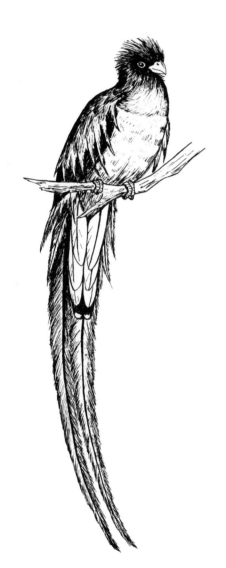

The famed quetzal (*Pharomachrus mocinno*) of Central America, highly prized by the Meso-American Indians for its beautiful green iridescent tail feathers. (Drawing by Yvonne Lee.)

family, the Zygodactylidae, is known from the Miocene of France and Germany, but its affinities are uncertain. Widespread during Cenozoic time, piciforms are now largely confined to the tropical regions of the Old and New Worlds, but are not represented in the Australian region, in Madagascar, or in Oceania. Climatic deterioration during late Cenozoic time, combined with competition from the more advanced perching birds, has left the woodpeckers as the piciforms' only representative in the temperate zone.

The primitive members of the order are the puffbirds (Bucconidae) and the jacamars (Galbulidae), which are often separated into a suborder, the Galbulae. They show numerous distinctions from the Pici, the suborder containing the remaining forms—honeyguides, barbets, toucans, and woodpeckers. Both puffbirds and jacamars are today confined to the neotropics. The 30 species of puffbirds are insectivorous forest birds living primarily in the Amazon Basin; the 14 species of jacamars are more commonly found at the edge of forests. Jacamars, like puffbirds, fly out from their perch to catch insects on the wing, and both excavate nest burrows in banks.

The evolutionary affinities of the piciforms have been thoroughly discussed by Charles Sibley and Jon Ahlquist of the Peabody Museum of Natural History at Yale University (1972, pp. 231–239), and the basic question is whether or not the Piciformes as currently defined is a monophyletic or a heterogeneous assemblage. It seems clear at least that the puffbird and jacamar families are quite distant from the other piciform families and are related to each other. They share a number of osteological characters with the primitive coraciiform families, externally closely resembling the Madagascan ground roller *Uratelornis*. In fact, these two families may well link the piciforms with ancient coraciiform ancestors. Their zygodactyl foot does not preclude such a relationship because zygodactyly has arisen independently a number of times in birds, and the cuckoo roller *Leptosomus* is facultatively zygodactyl, capable of reversing the outer toe at will.

It is clear also that the living Bucconidae, the puffbirds, show a very close affinity to the fossil forms of the North American Eocene family Primobucconidae (Feduccia and Martin, 1976). After studying the eight species of this ancient family, Larry Martin and I concluded that their appearance on the continent in the absence of other arboreal perching birds indicated that these zygodactyl forms were the predominant, if not the only, arboreal birds during the Eocene of North America. There is now also a primobucconid known from the Eocene of Europe; but this is not surprising because during the Eocene an Atlantic land bridge connected Europe with North America.

Of the Piciformes in the suborder Pici, perhaps the most intriguing are the honeyguides (Indicatoridae). They are confined to the Old World, with 9 of the 11 species occurring in Africa south of the Sahara

WALTER A WEBER

Coevolution of bird and mammal is illustrated by the association of the greater honeyguide (*Indicator indicator*) and the honey badger, as well as African man. The honeyguide leads the badger or man to a beehive, where the mammal reciprocates by tearing apart the beehive so that the honeyguide can gain access. Africans attract the attention of the honeyguides by grunting like the badger and chopping on trees to imitate the sound of opening a bees' nest. (From Friedmann, 1954; drawing by Walter A. Weber.)

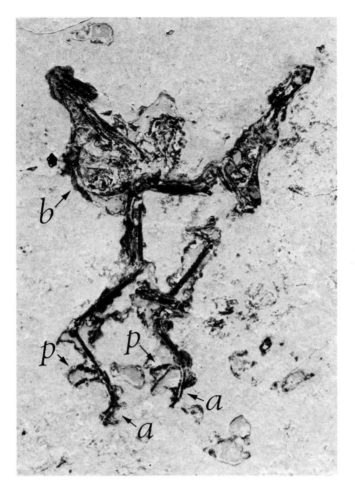

Left, fossil of the early Eocene primo-bucconid *Neanis kistneri* (Feduccia), a primitive, perching piciform bird from the Green River Formation of Wyoming. Its actual length in life was 4–5 inches. Abbreviations: *b*, braincase; *a*, anterior toes; *p*, posterior toes. Right, a living member of the structurally primitive piciform family Bucconidae (the pied puffbird, *Notharchus tectus*), now confined to the neotropics and thought to be closely allied to the North American Eocene fossil family Primobucconidae. Note the zygodactyl foot in both the living and fossil forms. (From Feduccia, 1977c.)

and the other 2 appearing in the Malayan region and the western Himalayas. This perching family gets its name from the extraordinary habit developed in some of the African species of leading the honey badger (or ratel) and African man to beehives. This mutualism rewards both parties, for in addition to feeding on bees and wasps, honeyguides practice the strange habit of eating wax. No species of honeyguide is known to build a nest; all practice brood parasitism, depositing their eggs in the nests of various host species. Newly hatched chicks are equipped with a calcareous hook on the tip of the bill that they use to kill their nestmates.

The barbets (Capitonidae) are a family of perching piciforms, some with large, broad bills, found in the tropics of both hemispheres. Barbets were once widespread, as is indicated by discoveries of fossils in the Miocene of Europe. They prefer to eat fruits and berries, but include some insects in their diet. Like other piciforms, barbets nest in tree cavities.

Derived from barbet ancestors are the neotropical toucans (Ramphastidae), characterized by the massive bills they use for eating fruit. Like barbets, toucans nest in tree cavities. They are somewhat convergent on the Old World tropical hornbills, and there is a smooth morphological gradation in bill size from the barbets through the toucanets to the toucans.

Unlike the toucans, the woodpeckers and allies (Picidae) are not traceable back to a specific group within the Piciformes. They are probably of late Tertiary origin, the oldest fossil woodpecker coming from the early Pliocene of North America. The success of the woodpeckers (subfamily Picinae), now spread throughout most of the world except Australia, is probably due to their acquisition of scansorial habits and their physiological adaptation to temperate-zone climates. The family also contains two smaller, less specialized groups, the wrynecks (subfamily Jynginae), confined to the Old World, and the tiny piculets (subfamily Picumninae), occurring in the tropics.

By far the most numerous group of living birds are the passerines, often referred to as songbirds. They constitute over 5,000 species, approximately three-fifths of all living birds. Most are small to medium-sized, but some, such as the raven and Australian lyrebird, are fairly large. During the late Tertiary the passerines were so successful that lines of demarcation between families and higher groups are very poorly defined, and the differences between many of the passerine families are not as great as those between nonpasserine genera. Instead of distinct evolutionary lines that can be traced by conventional methods, passerine phylogenies look like the upended head of an artist's paint brush with the myriad single strands inextricably mixed. So poorly understood are passerine family boundaries that students of the group may use as few as 50 or as many as 70 families to accommodate the various species.

The term "songbirds" was invented by people living in the temperate zones, and referred initially only to the suborder Passeres of the order Passeriformes—the oscines—the noted songsters of the temperate zones. The oscines constitute about four-fifths of the passerine birds. The rest are called suboscines, and the vast majority of them are classified in the suborder Tyranni, a group of New World birds prominent in the neotropics, especially in the deepest regions of Amazonia. The most familiar of these forms outside the tropics are the New World flycatchers (family Tyrannidae); many species of these flycatchers migrate north from the tropics, their ancestral homeland, to the temperate zone, to nest in the summer, returning to the tropics in the winter. There are also several relict groups of Old World suboscines, including the broadbills, pittas, and philepittas, whose classification into suborders is uncertain.

These two major groups of songbirds, the oscines and suboscines, are united into the single order Passeriformes by a particular arrangement of the palatal bones, termed aegithognathous, and by their sperm structure, to mention only a few common features. The two suborders have been distinguished from each other by detailed anatomical anal-

The structurally diverse living perching piciform birds. Center, keel-billed toucan (*Ramphastos sulfuratus*), family Ramphastidae, now confined to the New World tropics; upper right, the collared puffbird (*Bucco capensis*), family Bucconidae, also confined to the New World tropics; upper left, the great jacamar (*Jacamerops aurea*), family Galbulidae, confined to the New World tropics; lower left, the toucan barbet (*Semnornis ramphastinus*), family Capitonidae, restricted to the tropics in both the Old and New Worlds; and lower center, the greater honeyguide (*Indicator indicator*), family Indicatoridae, restricted primarily to Africa. (Drawing by Melissa Marshall.)

The varied members of the advanced piciform family Picidae, a family adapted primarily for tree-trunk foraging. Top, the red-headed woodpecker (*Melanerpes erythrocephalus*), subfamily Picinae, of nearly cosmopolitan distribution; middle, a piculet (*Picumnus rufiventris*), subfamily Picumninae, of the Old and New World tropics; bottom, the wryneck (*Jyux torquilla*), subfamily Jynginae, of Eurasia and Africa. (Drawing by Melissa Marshall.)

ysis of the musculature of the voice box, or syrinx. Suboscines all have
simple syringes, while the oscines have more than three pairs of intrinsic syringeal muscles. On the whole, oscine songs appear to be much
more complex than the songs of the suboscines. A German anatomist,
Johannes Müller, studied the muscles of the syrinx over a century ago
(1847) and subdivided the entire passerine assemblage on the basis of
this structure, placing the suboscines into several suborders, and the
oscines into the single suborder Passeres. Peter Ames (1971) recently
restudied the passerine syrinx in great detail and found that the oscine
syrinx is complex but uniform throughout the suborder, suggesting a
narrowly monophyletic group. He found suboscines to have simpler
syringes, but he also found the structure to be highly variable
throughout the group. He concluded that taxonomic decisions based
on the syringes would have to be made very cautiously, and that bas-
ing the unity of the suboscines on the simple syringes was not satisfactory. If simple syringeal morphology was, as it seemed, a retained
primitive characteristic, it would not be suitable evidence for establishing evolutionary relationships. However, more recent studies of the
middle-ear ossicle have shown persuasively that the suboscines are, in
fact, a tight, monophyletic group. All of the suboscines in both the
Old and New Worlds are characterized by a stapes with a large, bulbous footplate region, resembling that of the alcediniform birds, but
differing in specific details. Oscines, in contrast, have a simple stapes
with a flat, oval footplate.

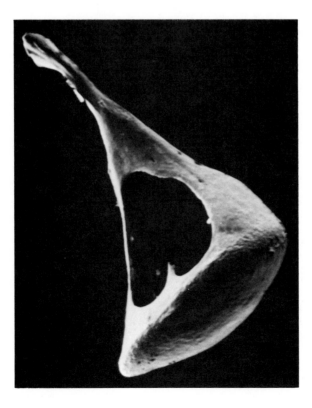

A scanning electron micrograph of the
stapes of a South American ovenbird
(*Furnarius rufus*), a New World suboscine, showing the middle-ear ossicle
characteristic of all suboscine birds.
(From Feduccia, 1974b.)

There are a number of characters of suboscines other than the simple syrinx that are clearly primitive within the passerine assemblage: the lack of a sternal spine in some forms, a simple scapula, the primitive single (as opposed to double) fossa of the humerus in all species. In addition, the sperm of the suboscines are not as complex as those of oscines (Feduccia, 1979).

The oscines represent an absolute extreme among birds, and perhaps all living vertebrates, in their morphological uniformity. All have a nearly identical syringeal structure, as we have seen, a very similar pattern of feather tracts, and the simple, primitive type of middle-ear ossicle. Most are small land birds primarily adapted for feeding on insects, small fruits, and seeds, and therefore many of the differences we do see among them are in the feeding mechanism and bill, structures that are often convergent rather than indicative of evolutionary relationship. The lack of major gaps between the various oscine families suggests that the adaptive radiation of modern, advanced oscines is probably very recent, perhaps having occurred in the middle to late Tertiary.

Two of the few important characteristics that have been used classically to separate the oscines are the form of the proximal end of the humerus and the number of primary feathers. The primitive type of humerus has only a single fossa, or excavation at the proximal end; this style of humerus is found in many oscines (and in all of the suboscines, piciforms, and coraciiforms), but other oscine groups have the advanced double fossa. In flying birds the number of primary feathers varies from 9 to 12, but in passerine birds there are typically 10. In some oscines, however, the tenth (or outermost) primary is reduced to a vestigial feather, and these birds are referred to as nine-primaried. Obviously, the nine-primaried state is the derived condition within the oscines.

There have been two schools of thought concerning the competitive relations between the oscines and suboscines. The most recent school, whose principal advocates are Paul Slud (1960) and Edwin Willis (1966), maintains that the suboscines are not actually primitive within the passerine assemblage, and hold their own against competition from oscines. These conclusions are based on the fact that suboscines are a very successful group of birds in South America in terms of adaptive radiation of morphological types and species numbers; and according to Willis, suboscines seem to be behaviorally adept in competing with winter oscine migrants in the tropics. The other school, which I shall follow here, represents the classical view and has been championed by Ernst Mayr and Dean Amadon (1951; also see Amadon, 1973). It argues that suboscines are indeed more primitive and have been replaced by the more advanced oscines wherever the two groups have been in competition.

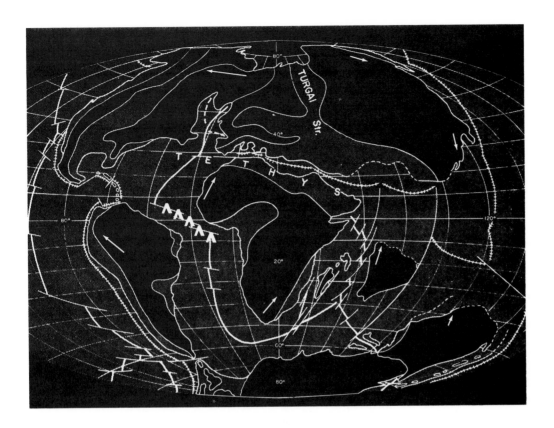

The oscines and suboscines surely had an ancient common ancestor. According to the classical view of Amadon and Mayr, the suboscines represent a "first attempt" at becoming a highly advanced passerine bird, becoming widespread some time before the mid-Tertiary. The oscines, by contrast, did not undergo any extensive evolution until later in the Tertiary.

Suboscine ancestors were present in the ancient southern continent of Gondwanaland before the separation of South America and Africa. After the continents began to drift apart in the late Cretaceous, the ancestral suboscines easily could have continued their dispersal across the then very narrow Atlantic Ocean, which even as late as the Paleocene separated the two land masses by perhaps no more than 375 miles—the equivalent distance of the trans–Gulf of Mexico migration route used today by the suboscine tyrant flycatchers. Also, at that time the mid-Atlantic ridge probably was dotted with volcanic islands that could have provided way stations for the dispersal (Raven and Axelrod, 1975). We can assume, then, an extensive Southern Hemisphere adaptive radiation of suboscines.

In the New World, the Central American land bridge had not yet come into being and South America existed in isolation from North America. Even in mid-Tertiary times, when climates were quite mild, there was no opportunity for New World suboscines to venture north.

Reconstruction of the continents in the late Cretaceous, approximately 65 million years ago. Note the volcanic island arcs indicated in the mid-Atlantic. (Adapted from Rich, 1975.)

Oscine bones from the upper Pliocene deposits of the Rexroad Formation in western Kansas. Hundreds of passerine bones have been recovered from North American Pliocene deposits, and all of them represent oscines. (Photo by the author.)

In the Old World, however, no geographic barriers existed, and the radiation of suboscines extended well into the north, as is indicated by a fossil broadbill from the Miocene of Europe.

In the middle to late Tertiary, the oscines began an extensive adaptive radiation that edged out the suboscines wherever the two groups came into competition, as they frequently did in the Old World. In the late Tertiary the oscines apparently used the Bering land bridge to invade the New World Northern Hemisphere. But until recently, the oscines remained isolated in North America, while the suboscines thrived in South America, where there are about 1,000 species, contained in 9 families in a wide variety of body forms. It is this flourishing of suboscines in South America that led Slud and Willis to question the classical view of suboscine-oscine competition. However, a closer examination of the evidence tends to lessen the impression of suboscine success. Clearly, suboscines did not break out of South America until the late Pliocene. With the exception of tyrant flycatchers, suboscines are absent from the West Indies. The suboscines of Trinidad are not endemic and represent a recent invasion from South America at a time when the island was connected with that continent during the Pleistocene. The Central American suboscines are undoubtedly extralimital members of South American superspecies groups that have recently moved north. In addition, the fossil record indicates that there were no suboscines in North America even as late as 3.8 million years ago, even though the Central American land bridge has existed for 5.7 million years. Given the moderate climates of the late Pliocene and Pleistocene in North America, it seems reasonable to assume that the suboscines, if present, would have undergone an extensive radiation.

One of the thousands of oscines, the African superb starling (*Spreo superba,* family Sturnidae). (Photo by the author.)

During the late Pliocene advanced mammals crossed the land bridge into South America and precipitated a massive wave of extinction in the archaic fauna of that continent. The suboscines survived despite the late Pliocene invasion of oscines from North America, but the significance of this persistence diminishes when other factors are considered. In the very late Tertiary the major Andean uplift occurred, causing major topographic changes and creating new life zones, including the deserts along the west coast, into which suboscines could radiate. Also, as Jürgen Haffer has shown (1969, 1974), Pleistocene fluctuations of humid and dry periods in the vast Amazon Basin resulted in rapid speciation in the birds of the region, including the suboscines.

It is this recent extensive speciation, combined with the very recent and diverse speciation that occurred in the new habitats created by the Andean uplift, that has provided the suboscines with such an image of success when compared with the oscines. But as Dean Amadon carefully summarizes, "All in all, I see no reason to abandon the classical view that the sub-Oscines are an early and in general less well-adapted group of Passeriformes that has persisted in South America longer than elsewhere because it was sheltered from the main wave of Oscine evolution" (1973, p. 274).

The nearly 4,000 species of oscines constitute almost half of the living birds of the world, but because of their extreme morphological similarity, efforts to categorize them have been fraught with much more difficulty than the taxonomy of suboscines. In 1888 the famed anatomist Maximillian Fürbringer actually recognized only 2 oscine families; then in 1934 the distinguished ornithologist Erwin Stresemann recognized 49; and Alexander Wetmore in 1960 recognized 54, a number approximating today's usage. To avoid detailed discussion here of the intricacies of oscine classification, I shall merely outline some major groupings. One fairly well recognized group is the corvine assemblage, which includes the crows and jays, bowerbirds, and birds-of-paradise. These birds have been placed both at the beginning and the end of the oscines in different classifications. They have been placed last because of the supposedly higher mental capabilities exhibited by the corvids and of the highly complex behavior and plumage seen in the bowerbirds and birds-of-paradise. Contrarily, they have been placed at the beginning of the oscine classification because of their primitive structural features, all of them having 10 primaries and the primitive type of humerus. Another major category is the predominantly Old World group of ten-primaried oscines, including Old World warblers, Old World flycatchers, babblers, and thrushes, and New World groups such as the wrens and mimids. A third major grouping, generally considered to be the most advanced, consists of the so-called New World nine-primaried oscines. This predominantly New World group includes the vireos, wood warblers, tanagers, icterids, and the emberizine and cardueline finches. In 1970 Charles Sibley accurately summarized our understanding of the New World nine-primaried oscines: "This cumbersome and not wholly accurate phrase is sanctioned by custom to designate a large assemblage of passerine birds. They are not confined to the New World, although more numerous there in terms of species, and some passerines with nine primaries are not included. The confusion is compounded because there is no agreement about the boundaries of the group" (pp. 98–99).

Given such groupings, it is not difficult to understand why the oscine story is still in total confusion. Recently, Robert Raikow of the University of Pittsburgh has begun a careful study of the musculature of the oscines in an attempt to establish a phylogeny (see Raikow, 1978). And several biochemical studies now being conducted promise to yield information that will increase our understanding of these puzzling birds. Charles Sibley's research on DNA hybridization at Yale University may well be of great importance in elucidating oscine relationships, and a variety of biochemical studies being conducted by Allan C. Wilson and his colleagues at the University of California at Berkeley will no doubt contribute greatly to the systematic evaluation of many avian groups, including the oscines.

Suboscine taxonomic categories are more clearly defined. In the Old World these birds are represented by three distinctive families of perching birds that have managed to hang on to their peculiar niches in the face of oscine competition. These relicts are now distributed erratically throughout the tropical regions. A structurally primitive group of suboscines is the broadbill family (Eurylaimidae), which is composed of 14 brightly colored species of insectivorous, carnivorous (eating small frogs and lizards), and frugivorous birds. They construct a purselike hanging nest of grasses and other fibers with the entrance hole approximately in the center. Broadbills range erratically across tropical Africa, and occur in Asia from the Himalayan foothill region to the Philippines and on to Sumatra and Borneo. There is a fossil broadbill from the Miocene of Bavaria (Ballmann, 1969b), indicating that the group was once much more widespread.

The other major group of Old World suboscine birds is the pittas (family Pittidae). Chubby birds with unusually short tails that are often not apparent at a distance, pittas are brightly colored, with different forms displaying a wide variety of greens, reds, purples, and yellows. The 23 species are placed in the same genus, *Pitta,* indicating the homogeneity of the group. All inhabit the lower regions and floors of moist tropical forests, and in their habitat and body form they are highly convergent with the New World tropical antpittas and some of the antbirds. Pittas feed almost entirely on earthworms and build a large globular nest with an entrance hole on one side. The center of their distribution is southeastern Asia and Malaysia, but two species are confined to central and east Africa, and four species have invaded Australia. Their relictual distribution across the Old World tropics is reminiscent of that of the broadbills; but unlike the broadbills, a number of pittas are migratory, nesting as far north as China and Japan and returning to the tropics for the winter.

The only other remnants of the Old World suboscine radiation are the two species of asities (genus *Philepitta*) and two of false sunbirds (genus *Neodrepanis*) of the family Philepittidae. Like many other primitive animals, they survive today only on the island refugium of Madagascar. The asities are small, plump arboreal birds that superficially resemble the pittas, while the false sunbirds are convergent with the more recently evolved oscine sunbird family Nectariniidae, which contains 115 species and is widely distributed across Africa, Asia, Australia, and adjacent regions. These small birds, like the true sunbirds, dip their recurved bills into flowers to obtain nectar and small insects. A nest is known only for the velvet asity, a woven hanging structure with a side entrance.

The New World suboscines are divided on the basis of syringeal architecture into two superfamilies: the Tyrannoidea, containing the flycatchers, sharpbills, plant cutters, cotingas, and manakins; and the Furnarioidea, containing the ovenbirds and woodhewers, antbirds and tapaculos. Most numerous and best known of the New World suboscines are the 365 species of tyrant flycatchers (family Tyrannidae). These are primarily arboreal insect-eaters, with rather broad bills surrounded by special feathers modified as bristles that aid in capturing insects. In South America some forms have become largely terrestrial and have come to resemble larks or pipits. Many tyrant flycatchers are remarkably similar, at least superficially, to the Old World flycatchers of the large oscine family Muscicapidae, containing 398 species. Both

the Old and New World flycatchers have similar habits, and capture insects on the wing by making short sallies from a prominent perch. A number of New World flycatchers migrate into North America for nesting during the summer, but generally return to the tropics for the winter, although some winter in the southern United States.

Several small groups of South American suboscines appear to be closely related to the flycatchers, but are generally treated as separate families. There is only a single species of the sharpbill (Oxyruncidae), represented mostly by scattered specimens in museums. These have been collected in six countries ranging from Costa Rica to Brazil, but no one has observed this species enough in the wild to learn its habits. The three species of plant cutters (Phytotomidae), so called because they use their saw-toothed bills for cutting plant material for food, occur in temperate South America from western Peru to Patagonia. The 90 species of cotingas (Cotingidae) are structurally primitive and resemble the Old World broadbills, but the similarity is certainly due to the fact that both groups have broadened bills adapted for fruit-eating. This heterogeneous family includes such bizarre forms as the bell-birds, fruit-crows, umbrella birds, cocks of the rock, becards, and many more, most of which have striking and often gaudily colored plumage. The becards (15 species) have been thought by some to be flycatchers. One form, the Jamaican becard, is the only cotinga to get into the West Indies; and the northernmost species, the rose-throated becard, nests as far north as the southwestern United States. Many cotinga species are exceptionally large, and the cock of the rock (12 inches) is a deep-forest form that has evolved courtship behavior in which the gaudy males display for the drab females on special territories called leks or arenas.

The 59 species of manakins (family Pipridae) are a homogeneous group of small suboscines, usually not exceeding 5 inches in length. Many have thought manakins are closely related to the cotingas, probably because, like cotingas, manakin males are exceptionally brightly

The diverse families of the suboscines, united by their common possession of a unique type of middle-ear ossicle (center). The major families of New World suboscines are on the left and at the lower center; the families of Old World suboscines are on the right. Left, from top to bottom, the yellow-thighed manakin (*Pipra mentalis*), family Pipridae; the gray gallito (*Rhinocrypta lanceolata*), family Rhinocryptidae; the plain xenops (*Xenops minutus*), family Furnariidae; the scaled antpitta (*Grallaria guatamalensis*), family Formicariidae; the masked tityra (*Tityra semi-fasciata*), family Cotingidae; and lower center, the great kiskadee (*Pitangus surphuratus*), family Tyrannidae. Right, from top to bottom, the velvet asity (*Philepitta castanea*) and the wattled false sunbird (*Neodrepanis coruscans*), family Philepittidae; Steere's pitta (*Pitta steerii*), family Pittidae; and the black and yellow broadbill (*Eurylaimus ochromalus*), family Eurylaimidae. Note that the New World antpittas are highly convergent with the Old World pittas, as are the New World cotingas with the Old World broadbills. (Drawing by Melissa Marshall.)

colored and display on leks to attract the unprepossessing females, but the evidence for affinity is inconclusive. Many manakins have special modifications of the wing feathers that produce strange rattles and buzzing noises in flight.

The 263 species of ovenbirds and woodhewers (Furnariidae) constitute an extremely diverse family of small- to medium-sized, mainly brownish birds that range in habit from being completely terrestrial to being completely scansorial. The 48 species of woodhewers are often placed in a separate family, the Dendrocolaptidae; they spend their lives hitching up tree trunks in search of food, and in appearance and habits closely resemble the unrelated temperate zone oscine family Certhiidae, the brown creepers. Ovenbirds are not related to the oscine wood warbler that is often called an ovenbird; they are so named for several species that build a domed, clay nest shaped like an old-fashioned earth oven. Most, however, dig tunnels in banks or build an open-cup nest. The ovenbirds are insectivorous, and a large number of species glean their food from deep-forest foliage. So morphologically different are the various members of the ovenbird family that it may be the most diverse of all the passerine families.

Another extremely large suboscine family of primarily deep-forest, insectivorous birds is composed of the antbirds (Formicariidae), like the ovenbirds and woodhewers most abundant in the Amazon Basin. Antbirds exhibit a great variety of adaptive types, ranging from the wrenlike antwrens to the shrikelike antshrikes, and on to the pitta-like antpittas, which very closely resemble the fully terrestrial Old World suboscine pittas. Most antpittas build a simple cup nest in branches near the ground. The antpipits, or gnateaters (*Conophaga*), are often included in this family; they are small, completely terrestrial forest birds that closely resemble the antpittas of the genus *Grallaria*.

The 26 species of tapaculos of the family Rhinocryptidae are a relict family of primitive suboscine birds now found mostly in the Andean region of Chile. Tapaculos are insectivorous, terrestrial or semi-terrestrial, nonmigratory birds that are mainly confined to scrublands or the thick undergrowth of high mountain forests. Their nests range from tunnels in banks to bulky, domed constructions of grasses. Most species have a very poorly developed flight apparatus, often almost entirely lacking the sternal keel and having greatly reduced, unfused clavicles. Storrs Olson and I (Feduccia and Olson, in preparation) have shown that the tapaculos exhibit numerous primitive skeletal features, including a four-notched sternum and a humerus resembling that of primitive coraciiforms, and some have a primitive stapes.

The tapaculos are in some ways morphologically similar to two relict groups of oscines, the lyrebirds and scrub-birds. Over a hundred years ago the lyrebirds (Menuridae) and the tapaculos were included in the same family, but because of their enormously disjunct geographic distribution, they are now considered by most authors to be conver-

Relict, primitive oscines: a male Australian lyrebird (*Menura*), left; the Australian scrub-bird (*Atrichornis*), right. (Drawings by Sigrid K. James.)

gent. The two species of lyrebirds, noted for their elongated tail feathers, are residents of forests and scrublands in eastern Australia; they are largely terrestrial, running through undergrowth, but occasionally take to flight. Their food consists largely of insects, worms, and a variety of crustaceans. The male establishes a display territory, and the female alone builds the nest, a massive domed structure with a side entrance. The two species of scrub-birds (Atrichornithidae) are small, primarily insectivorous birds that are restricted to the scrublands of small regions of southwestern and southeastern Australia. They build a small version of the lyrebird's domed nest, but little else is known of their habits. Lyrebirds and scrub-birds are clearly the most primitive of the oscines.

Another enigmatic group of primitive, living oscines is the New Zealand wrens of the family Acanthisittidae. The four species of these small wrenlike birds were long thought to be of suboscine rather than oscine affinity, but it now seems clear that these forms represent another oscine line, quite removed from the lyrebird–scrub-bird group, that still persists relictually in New Zealand.

Though far from perfect, our knowledge of land birds does allow us to construct a very generalized history of their rise and dispersion. A number of waves of evolution seem to have characterized the appearance of at least the more advanced arboreal land birds, each wave fleetingly successful, and each one finally leaving a handful of relics in the modern avifauna. Arboreal piciforms were the predominant, if not the only, perching birds during the Eocene of North America and possibly Eurasia, but we do not know how piciform evolution was then

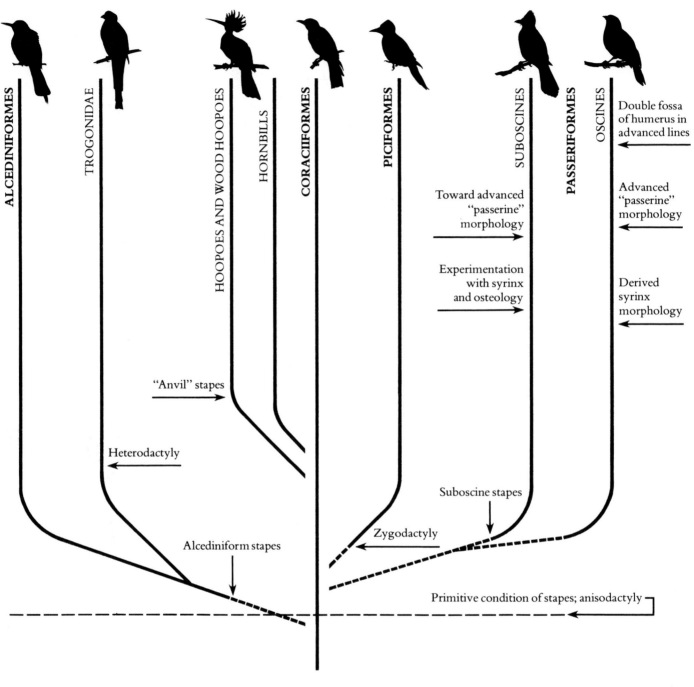

Hypothetical family tree of the coraciiforms, piciforms, and passeriforms. The ancient coraciiform birds, similar to living relicts on Madagascar such as the ground rollers and cuckoo rollers, probably were the progenitors of many modern arboreal birds. Living coraciiforms include the true rollers, shown at top center, hornbills, and the hoopoes and wood hoopoes. One group of "coraciiforms," now placed in the separate order Alcediniformes, is characterized by a unique type of middle-ear ossicle, and one of its families, the Trogonidae, has reversed the inner toe to become heterodactyl. Piciform birds, instead, reversed the outer toe to become zygodactyl. The oscines and suboscines shared an ancient common ancestor, and the suboscines, though not as structurally advanced as the oscines in many features, are characterized by a unique type of middle-ear ossicle. (Adapted from Feduccia, 1977c.)

proceeding in other parts of the world. The Oligocene seems to have been an equally successful period for the coraciiform birds. Having originated (possibly in earlier times) in the Old World, probably in Eurasia, they underwent extensive radiation in the Oligocene, and possibly at that time, invaded the New World across the Bering land bridge. The suboscines were no doubt a Gondwanaland group; their distribution, especially in the New World, indicates confinement to South America until the establishment of the Central American land bridge. Ancestral oscines apparently arose in the Old World, and in the middle to late Tertiary, upon the eventual evolution of advanced forms, they outcompeted their Old World suboscine counterparts wherever they came into contact, leaving today only a few suboscine relics exhibiting a broad range of morphological types. Repeated invasions of oscines into the New World across the Bering land bridge produced the myriad of families present today, probably after the early Miocene. The New World apparently did not reciprocate to any significant degree with its newly evolved oscine stock. The Miocene of Eurasia was characterized by an avifauna that is today typical of Ethiopia; or to put it another way, the present-day fauna of Africa south of the Sahara is a relict Eurasian avifauna. Late Tertiary climatic deterioration, combined with competition from advanced oscine counterparts, forced the more primitive tropical arboreal land birds, such as the perching piciforms and coraciiforms, southward into the tropical regions. In the New World the closing of the Panamanian seaway and the concomitant establishment of the Central American land bridge in Pliocene time led to the extensive radiation of many birds. The Central American alcediniform birds, such as the trogons and motmots, entered South America; the South American suboscines moved northward; and, perhaps most important, the oscines invaded the neotropics, where they are now firmly established.

Bibliography

Amadon, D. 1947. An estimated weight of the largest known bird. *Condor* 49:159–164.

———1973. Birds of the Congo and Amazon forests: a comparison. In *Tropical forest ecosystems in Africa and South America: a comparative review*, ed. E. S. Ayensu and W. D. Duckworth, pp. 267–277. Washington, D.C., Smithsonian Institution Press.

Ames, P. L. 1971. The morphology of the syrinx in passerine birds. *Bulletin of the Peabody Museum of Natural History, Yale University* 37:1–194.

Andrews, C. W. 1896. Note on a nearly complete skeleton of *Aptornis defossor* Owen. *The Geological Magazine* 96:241–242.

Archey, G. 1941. The moa: a study of the Dinornithiformes. *Bulletin of the Auckland Institute and Museum* 1:1–145.

Arrendondo, O. 1976. The great predatory birds of the Pleistocene of Cuba. *Smithsonian Contributions to Paleobiology* 27:169–187.

Austin, O. L. Jr. *Birds of the world: a survey of the twenty-seven orders and one hundred and fifty-five families.* New York, Golden Press.

Bakker, R. T. 1975. Dinosaur renaissance. *Scientific American* 232(4):58–78.

Ballmann, P. 1969a. Les oiseaux miocènes de la Grive-Saint-Alben (Isère). *Geobios* 2:147–204.

———1969b. Die Vögel aus der altburdiagalen Spaltenfüllung von Wintershoft (West) bei Eichstätt in Bayern. *Zitteliana* 1:5–60.

Beebe, C. W. 1915. A tetrapteryx stage in the ancestry of birds. *Zoologica* 2:39–52.

Benton, M. J. 1979. Ectothermy and the success of dinosaurs. *Evolution* 33:983–997.

Bock, W. J. 1963. The cranial evidence for ratite affinities. *Proceedings of the Eighth International Ornithological Congress*, pp. 39–54.

———1965. The role of adaptive mechanisms in the origin of the higher levels of organization. *Systematic Zoology* 14:272–287.

Bond, J. 1966. Affinities of the Antillean avifauna. *Caribbean Journal of Science* 6:173–176.

Bouvier, M. 1977. Dinosaur Haversian bone and endothermy. *Evolution* 31:449–450.

Brasil, L. 1914. *Grues.* Pt. 26 of *Genera Avium*, ed. W. Wytsman. Brussels, V. Verteneuil.

Brodkorb, P. 1963. A giant flightless bird from the Pleistocene of Florida. *Auk* 80:111–115.

———1967. Catalogue of fossil birds: Part 3 (Ralliformes, Ichthyornithiformes, Charadriiformes). *Bulletin of the Florida State Museum* 11:99–220.

———1971. Origin and evolution of birds. In *Avian biology*, ed. D. S. Farner and J. R. King, pp. 19–55. New York, Academic Press.

———1976. Discovery of a Cretaceous bird, apparently ancestral to the order Coraciiformes and Piciformes (Aves: Carinatae). 27:67–73.

Broom, R. 1913. On the South African pseudosuchian *Euparkeria* and allied genera. *Proceedings of the Zoological Society of London* 1913:619–633.

Burger, R., K. Ducate, K. Robinson, and H. Walter. 1975. Radiocarbon date for the largest extinct bird. *Nature* 258:709.

Burton, P. J. K. 1974. Jaw and tongue

features in Psittaciformes and other orders with special reference to the anatomy of the tooth-billed pigeon (*Dicunculus strigirostris*). *Journal of Zoology* 174:255–276.

Campbell, K. E., Jr., and E. P. Tonni. 1980. A new genus of teratorn from the Huayquerian of Argentina (Aves: Teratornithidae). *Los Angeles County Museum Contributions to Science,* in press.

Chandler, A. C. 1916. A study of the structure of feathers with reference to their taxonomic significance. *University of California Publications in Zoology* 13:243–446.

Colbert, E. H. 1969. *Evolution of the vertebrates.* 2nd ed. New York, John Wiley & Sons.

Condal, L. F. 1955. Notice preliminaire concernant la presence d'une plume d'Oiseau dans le Jurassique superieur du Montsech (Province de Lerida, Espagne). *Proceedings of the Eleventh International Ornithological Congress,* pp. 268–269.

Cottam, P. A. 1957. The pelecaniform characters of the skeleton of the shoe-bill stork *Balaeniceps rex. Bulletin of the British Museum (Natural History)* 5(3):51–72.

Cracraft, J. 1971. Caenagnathiformes: Cretaceous birds convergent in jaw mechanism to dicynodont reptiles. *Journal of Paleontology* 45:805–809.
———1972. A new Cretaceous charadriiform family. *Auk* 89:36–46.
———1974. Phylogeny and evolution of the ratite birds. *Ibis* 115:494–521.
———1976. The species of moas (Aves: Dinornithidae). *Smithsonian Contributions to Paleobiology* 27:189–205.

Cracraft, J., and P. V. Rich. 1972. Systematics and evolution of Cathartidae in the Old World Tertiary. *Condor* 74:272–283.

Dames, W. 1897. Ueber Brustbein, Schulter- und Beckengurtel der *Archaeopteryx. Sitzungsberiche preussische Akademische Wissenschaft* 2:818–834.

Darwin, C. 1934. *Charles Darwin's diary on the voyage of the H.M.S. "Beagle."* Ed. Nora Barlow. London, Cambridge University Press.
———1859. *On the origin of species by means of natural selection, or the preservation of favoured races in the struggle for life.* 2nd ed. London, John Murray.

De Beer, G. 1954. *Archaeopteryx lithographica: a study based on the British Museum specimen.* London, British Museum (Natural History).
———1956. The evolution of ratites. *Bulletin of the British Museum (Natural History)* 4:59–70.

De Flacourt, E. 1661. *Histoire de la grande isle Madagascar.* Paris.

Delacour, J., and D. Amadon. 1973. *Curassows and related birds.* New York, American Museum of Natural History Press.

Duff, R. 1949. *Pyramid Valley, Waikari, North Canterbury.* Christchurch, New Zealand.

Elzanowski, A. 1976. Palaeognathous bird from the Cretaceous of Central Asia. *Nature* 265:51–53.

Evans, J. 1865. On portions of a cranium and of a jaw, in the slab containing the fossil remains of the *Archaeopteryx. Natural History Review,* n.s., 5:415–421.

Ewer, R. F. 1965. The anatomy of the thecodont reptile *Euparkeria capensis* Broom. *Philosophical Transactions of the Royal Society of London* 176(2): 197–221.

Feduccia, A. 1973. Dinosaurs as reptiles. *Evolution* 27:166–169.
———1974a. Another Old World vulture from the New World. *The Wilson Bulletin* 86:251–255.
———1974b. Morphology of the bony stapes in New and Old World suboscines: new evidence for common ancestry. *Auk* 91:427–429.
———1975. *Morphology of the bony stapes (columella) in the Passeriformes and related groups: evolutionary implications.* University of Kansas, Publications of the Museum of Natural History, 63. Lawrence, Kansas.
———1976. Osteological evidence for the shorebird affinities of the flamingos. *Auk* 93:587–601.
———1977a. The whalebill is a stork. *Nature* 266(5604):710–720.
———1977b. Hypothetical stages in the evolution of modern ducks and flamingos. *Journal of Theoretical Biology* 67:715–721.
———1977c. A model for the evolution of perching birds. *Systematic Zoology* 26:19–31.
———1978. *Presbyornis* and the evolution of ducks and flamingos. *American Scientist* 66:298–304.
———1979. Comments on the phylogeny of perching birds. *Proceedings of the Biological Society of Washington* 92:689–696.

Feduccia, A., and P. McGrew. 1974. A flamingolike wader from the Eocene of Wyoming. *Contributions to Geology, University of Wyoming* 13(2):49–61.

Feduccia, A., and L. D. Martin. 1976. The Eocene zygodactyl birds of North America (Aves: Piciformes). *Smithsonian Contributions to Paleobiology* 27:101–110.

Feduccia, A., and H. B. Tordoff. 1979. Feathers of *Archaeopteryx*: asymmetric vanes indicate aerodynamic function. *Science* 203:1021–1022.

Fisher, J., and R. T. Peterson. 1964. *The world of birds.* Garden City, N.J., Doubleday.

Fjeldså, J. 1976. The systematic affinities of sandgrouses, Pteroclididae. *Videnskabelige Meddelelser Fra Dansk Naturhistorisk Forening* 139:179–243.

Fox, R. C. 1974. A middle Campanian, nonmarine occurrence of the Cretaceous toothed bird *Hesperornis* Marsh. *Canadian Journal of Earth Science* 11:1335–1338.

Friedmann, H. 1954. Honey-guide: the bird that eats wax. *National Geographic Magazine* 104:551–560.

Frith, H. J. 1967. *Waterfowl in Australia.* Honolulu, East-West Center Press.

Fürbringer, M. 1888. *Untersuchungen zur Morphologie und Systematik Vögel.* Amsterdam, Holkema.

Galton, P. M. 1970. Ornithischian dinosaurs and the origin of birds. *Evolution* 24:448–462.

George, J. C., and A. J. Berger. 1966. *Avian myology.* New York, Academic Press.

Gingerich, P. D. 1973. Skull of *Hesperornis* and early evolution of birds. *Nature* 243:70–73.
———1976. Evolutionary significance of the Mesozoic toothed birds. *Smithsonian Contributions to Paleo-*

biology 27:23–33.

Gould, J. 1852. On a new and most remarkable form in ornithology. *Proceedings of the Zoological Society of London* 1851:1–2.

Grayson, D. K. 1977. Pleistocene avifaunas and the overkill hypothesis. *Science* 195:691–693.

Gregory, J. T. 1951. Convergent evolution: the jaws of *Hesperornis* and the mosasaurs. *Evolution* 5:345–354.

———1952. The jaws of the Cretaceous toothed birds *Ichthyornis* and *Hesperornis*. *Condor* 54:73–89.

Haffer, J. 1969. Speciation in Amazonian forest birds. *Science* 65:131–137.

———1974. *Avian speciation in tropical South America, with a systematic survey of the toucans (Ramphastidae) and jacamars (Galbulidae)*. Publications of the Nuttall Ornithological Club, 14. Cambridge, Mass.

Harrison, C. J. O., and C. A. Walker. 1973. *Wyleyia*: a new bird humerus from the lower Cretaceous of England. *Paleontology* 16:721–728.

———1975. The Bradycnemidae, a new family of owls from the upper Cretaceous of Romania. *Paleontology* 18:563–570.

———1976. A reappraisal of *Prophaethon shrubsolei* Andrews (Aves). *Bulletin of the British Museum (Natural History) (Geology)* 27:30.

Heilmann, G. 1926. *The origin of birds*. London, Witherby.

Howard, H. 1947. California's flightless birds. *Los Angeles County Museum Quarterly* 6:7–11.

———1957. A gigantic "toothed" marine bird from the Miocene of California. *Santa Barbara Museum of Natural History Bulletin (Department of Geology)* 1:1–23.

———1966. A possible ancestor of the Lucas auk (family Mancallidae) from the Tertiary of Orange County, California. *Los Angeles County Museum Contributions to Science* 101:1–8.

———1970. A review of the extinct avian genus *Mancalla*. *Los Angeles County Museum Contributions to Science* 203:1–12.

Hurst, C. H. 1893. The digits in a bird's wing. *Natural Science News* 3:274–281.

Huxley, T. H. 1867. On the classification of birds and on the taxonomic value of the modifications of certain of the cranial bones observable in that class. *Proceedings of the Zoological Society of London* 1867:415–472.

———1868. On the animals which are most nearly intermediate between the birds and reptiles. *Annals and Magazine of Natural History* 2:66–75.

Johnston, P. A. 1979. Growth rings in dinosaur teeth. *Nature* 278:635–636.

Jollie, M. 1976. A contribution to the morphology and phylogeny of the Falconiformes. *Evolutionary Theory* 1:285–298.

Kahl, M. P. 1970. East Africa's magestic flamingos. *National Geographic Magazine* 137:276–294.

Kurochkin, E. N. 1976. A survey of the Paleogene birds of Asia. *Smithsonian Contributions to Paleobiology* 27:75–86.

Lambrecht, K. 1931. *Gallornis straeleni* n. g. n. sp. ein Kreidevogel aus Frankreich. *Bulletin du Musée Royal d'Histoire Naturelle de Belgique* 7(30):1–6.

———1933. *Handbuch der Palaeornithologie*. Berlin, Gebrüder Borntraeger.

Ligon, J. D. 1967. *Relationships of the cathartid vultures*. University of Michigan Museum of Zoology Occasional Papers, 651. Ann Arbor, Mich.

Lowe, P. R. 1928a. A description of *Atlantisia rogersi*, the diminutive flightless rail of Inaccessible Island (South Atlantic), with some notes on flightless rails. *Ibis*, 12th ser., 4:99–131.

———1928b. Studies and observations bearing on the phylogeny of the ostrich and its allies. *Proceedings of the Zoological Society of London* 1928:185–247.

———1933. On the primitive characters of the penguins and their bearing on the phylogeny of birds. *Proceedings of the Zoological Society of London* 1933 (pt. 2):483–538.

———1935. On the relationships of the Struthiones to the dinosaurs and to the rest of the avian class, with special reference to the position of *Archaeopteryx*. *Ibis*, 13th ser.,

5:298–429.

———1944. Some additional remarks on the phylogeny of the Struthiones. *Ibis* 86:37–42.

———1948. What are the Coraciiformes? *Ibis* 90:572–582.

Lucas, A. M., and P. R. Stettenheim. 1972. *Avian anatomy: Integument*. 2 vols. Agricultural Handbook no. 362. Washington, D.C., U.S. Government Printing Office.

Lucas, F. A. 1901. *Animals of the past*. New York, McClure Phillips.

McDowell, S. 1948. The bony palate of birds. Part I. The Paleognathae. *Auk* 65:520–549.

McGowen, T. 1972. *Album of dinosaurs*. Chicago: Rand McNally.

Maderson, P. F. A. 1972. On how an archosaurian scale might have given rise to an avian feather. *American Naturalist* 146:424–428.

Marsh, O. C. 1873. On a new subclass of fossil birds (Odontornithes). *American Journal of Science* 5:161–162.

———1877. Introduction and succession of vertebrate life in America. *American Journal of Science*, 3rd ser., 14:337–378.

———1880. *Odontornithes: a monograph on the extinct toothed birds of North America*. Report of the U.S. Geological Exploration of the Fortieth Parallel, no. 7. Washington, D.C.

———1881. Discovery of a fossil bird in the Jurassic of Wyoming. *American Journal of Science* 21:341–342.

Martin, L. D., and J. Tate, Jr. 1976. The skeleton of *Baptornis advenus* (Aves: Hesperornithiformes). *Smithsonian Contributions to Paleobiology* 27:35–66.

Martin, P. S. 1973. The discovery of America. *Science* 179:969–974.

Mayr, E. 1960. The emergence of evolutionary novelties. In *The evolution of life*, ed. S. Tax, pp. 349–380. Chicago, University of Chicago Press.

Mayr, E., and D. Amadon. 1951. A classification of recent birds. *American Museum Novitates* 1496:1–42.

Mayr, F. X. 1973. Ein Neuer *Archaeopteryx*-Fund. *Paläontologica Zeitschrift* 47:17–24.

Meyer, H. von. 1857. Beiträge zur näheren Kenntniss fossiler Reptilien. *Neues Jahrbuch fur Mineralogie, Geolo-*

gie, und Paläontologie 1857:532–543.

———1861. Vögel-Federn und *Palpipes pricus* von Solnhofen. *Neues Jahrbuch fur Mineralogie, Geologie, und Paläontologie* 1861:561.

Miller, L. H. 1916. Two vulturid raptors from the Pleistocene of Rancho La Brea. *University of California Publications, Department of Geology* 9:105–109.

Miller, L. H., and I. S. DeMay. 1942. The fossil birds of California: an avifauna and bibliography with annotations. *University of California Publications in Zoology* 47:47–142.

Mudge, B. F. 1879. Are birds derived from dinosaurs? *Kansas City Review of Science* 3:224–226.

Müller, J. 1847. *Uber die bisher unbekannten typischen Verschiedenheiten der Stimmorgane der Passerinen.* Abhandlungen Koniglich Akademie Wissenschaft. Berlin.

Newton, A. 1896. *A dictionary of birds.* London, Adam and Charles Black.

Nopcsa, F. von. 1907. Ideas on the origin of flight. *Proceedings of the Zoological Society of London* 1907:223–236.

Oliver, W. R. B. 1949. The moas of New Zealand and Australia. *Dominion Museum Bulletin* 15:1–206.

Olson, S. L. 1973. Evolution of the rails of the South Atlantic islands (Aves: Rallidae). *Smithsonian Contributions to Zoology* 152:1–53.

———1975a. *Ichthyornis* in the Cretaceous of Alabama. *The Wilson Bulletin* 87:103–105.

———1975b. Paleornithology of St. Helena Island, South Atlantic Ocean. *Smithsonian Contributions to Paleobiology* 23:1–49.

———1976. Oligocene fossils bearing on the origins of the Todidae and the Momotidae (Aves: Coraciiformes). *Smithsonian Contributions to Paleobiology* 27:111–119.

———1977a. A great auk, *Pinguinis*, from the Pliocene of North Carolina (Aves: Alcidae). *Proceedings of the Biological Society of Washington* 90:690–697.

———1977b. A lower Eocene frigatebird from the Green River Formation of Wyoming (Pelecaniformes: Frigatidae). *Smithsonian Contributions*

to Paleobiology 35:1–33.

———1979. Multiple origins of the Ciconiiformes. *Proceedings of the Colonial Waterbird Group* 1978:165–170.

Olson, S. L., and A. Feduccia. 1979. Flight capability and the pectoral girdle of *Archaeopteryx. Nature* 278(5701):247–248.

———1980a. Relationships and evolution of flamingos (Aves: Phoenicopteridae). *Smithsonian Contributions to Zoology,* in press.

———1980b. *Presbyornis* and the origin of the Anseriformes (Aves: Charadriomorphae). *Smithsonian Contributions to Zoology,* in press.

Olson, S. L., and Y. Hasegawa. 1979. Fossil counterparts of giant penguins from the North Pacific. *Science* 206:688–689.

Olson, S. L., and A. Wetmore. 1976. Preliminary diagnosis of two extraordinary new genera of birds from Pleistocene deposits in the Hawaiian Islands. *Proceedings of the Biological Society of Washington* 89:247–258.

Ostrom, J. H. 1970. *Archaeopteryx:* notice of a "new" specimen. *Science* 170:537–538.

———1974. *Archaeopteryx* and the origin of flight. *Quarterly Review of Biology* 49:27–47.

———1975. The origin of birds. *Annual Review of Earth and Planetary Science* 3:55–77.

———1976. Some hypothetical anatomical stages in the evolution of avian flight. *Smithsonian Contributions to Paleobiology* 27:1–21.

Owen, R. 1839. On the bone of an unknown Struthious bird from New Zealand. *Proceedings of the Zoological Society of London* 1839:169–170.

———1864. On the fossil remains of a longtailed bird, *Archaeopteryx macrura* from the lithographic slate of Solnhofen. *Proceedings of the Zoological Society of London* 12:272–273.

Parkes, K. C. 1966. Speculations on the origin of feathers. *Living Bird* 5:77–86.

Parkes, K. C., and G. A. Clark, Jr. 1966. An additional character linking ratites and tinamous, and an interpretation of their monophyly. *Condor* 68:459–471.

Peterson, R. T. 1963. *The birds.* Life Nature Library. New York, Time, Inc.

Petronievics, B. 1925. Über die Berliner *Archaeornis. Geologica Balkanskoga poluostrova* 8:37–84.

———1927. Nouvelles recherches sur l'ostéologie des Archaeornithes. *Annales Paleontologica* 16:39–55.

Polack, J. S. 1838. New Zealand. London, R. Bentley.

Pycraft, W. P. 1894. Wing of *Archaeopteryx. Journal of the Oxford University Junior Science Club* 1:172–176.

Raikow, R. J. 1970. Evolution of diving adaptations in the stifftail ducks. *University of California Publications in Zoology* 94:1–52.

———1978. Appendicular myology and relationships of the New World nine-primaried oscines (Aves: Passeriformes). *Bulletin of the Carnegie Museum of Natural History* 7:1–52.

Raven, P. H., and D. I. Axelrod. 1975. History of the flora and fauna of Latin America. *American Scientist* 63:420–429.

Rawles, M. E. 1960. The integumentary system. In *Biology and comparative physiology of birds,* ed. A. J. Marshall, vol. 1, pp. 189–240. New York, Academic Press.

Regal, P. J. 1975. The evolutionary origin of feathers. *Quarterly Review of Biology* 50:35–66.

Rich, P. V. 1975. Changing continental arrangements and the origin of Australia's non-passeriform continental avifauna. *Emu* 75:97–112.

———1979. *The Dromornithidae.* Bureau of Mineral Resources (Geology and Geophysics) Bulletin 184. Canberra, Australian Government Publishing Service.

Rich, P. V., and D. J. Bohaska. 1976. The world's oldest owl: a new strigiform from the Paleocene of southwestern Colorado. *Smithsonian Contributions to Paleobiology* 27:87–93.

Ripley, S. D. 1977. *Rails of the world.* Boston, Godine.

Romer, A. S. 1966. *Vertebrate paleontology.* 3rd ed. Chicago, University of Chicago Press.

Russell, D. A. 1967. Cretaceous vertebrates from the Anderson River,

N.W.T. *Canadian Journal of Earth Science* 4:21–38.

Sauer, E. G. F. 1976. Aepyornithoid eggshell fragments from the Miocene and Pliocene of Anatolia, Turkey. *Palaeontographica* 153:62–115.

Sauer, E. G. F., and P. Rothe. 1972. Ratite eggshells from Lanzarote, Canary Islands. *Science* 176:43–45.

Savile, D. B. O. 1957. Adaptive evolution in the avian wing. *Evolution* 11:212–224.

———1962. Gliding and flight in the vertebrates. *American Zoologist* 2:161–166.

Schinz, H. R., and R. Zangerl. 1937. Beiträge zur Osteogenese des Knochensystems beim Haushuhn, bei der Haustaube und beim Haubenseissfuss. *Denkshriften der Schweizerischen Naturforschenden Gesellschaft* 77:117–164.

Sibley, C. G. 1970. A comparative study of the egg-white proteins of passerine birds. *Bulletin of the Peabody Museum of Natural History, Yale University* 32:1–131B.

Sibley, C. G., and J. E. Ahlquist. 1972. A comparative study of the egg-white proteins of non-passerine birds. *Bulletin of the Peabody Museum of Natural History, Yale University* 39:1–276.

Simonetta, A. M. 1960. On the mechanical implications of the avian skull and their bearing on the evolution and classification of birds. *Quarterly Review of Biology* 35:206–220.

Simpson, G. G. 1946. Fossil penguins. *Bulletin of the American Museum of Natural History* 87:1–100.

———1975. Fossil penguins. In *The biology of penguins,* ed. Bernard Stonehouse, pp. 19–41. London, Macmillan.

———1976. *Penguins: past and present, here and there.* New Haven, Yale University Press.

Slud, P. 1960. The birds of Finca "La Selva," Costa Rica: a tropical wet forest locality. *Bulletin of the American Museum of Natural History* 128:49–148.

Stock, C. 1961. *Rancho La Brea: a record of Pleistocene life.* Los Angeles County Museum of Science Series, 20 (Paleontology, no. 11). Los Angeles.

Storer, R. W. 1956. The fossil loon *Colymboides minutus. Condor* 58:413–426.

———1960. Evolution in the diving birds. *Proceedings of the Twelfth International Ornithological Congress,* pp. 694–707.

Stresemann, E. 1934. *Aves.* Vol. 7, pt. 2, of *Handbuch de Zoologie,* ed. W. Kukenthal and T. Krumbach. Berlin, Walter de Gruyter.

Strickland, H. E. 1849. Supposed existence of a giant bird in Madagascar. *Annals and Magazine of Natural History,* 2nd ser., 4:338–339.

Sy, M. 1936. Funktionall-anatomische Untersuchungen am Vögelflugel. *Journal für Ornithologie* 84:199–296.

Talent, J. A., P. M. Duncan, and P. L. Handley. 1966. Early Cretaceous feathers from Victoria. *Emu* 66:81–86.

Tracy, C. R. 1976. Tyrannosaurs: evidence for endothermy? *American Naturalist* 110:1105–1106.

Van Tyne, J., and A. J. Berger. 1976. *Fundamentals of ornithology.* 2nd ed. New York, John Wiley & Sons.

Wagner, J. A. 1861a. Ueber ein neues, augenblich mit Vogelfedern versehenes Reptil aus dem Solenhofener lithographischen Schiefer. *Sitzungsberichte der Bayerischen Akademie der Wissenschaften* 2:146–154.

———1861b. Neue Beitrage zur Kenntnis der Urweltlichen Fauna des lithographisches Schiefers; V. *Compsognathus longipes* Wagner. *Abhandlungen Bayerischen Akademische Wissen-*
schaft 9:30–38.

———1862. On a new fossil reptile supposed to be furnished with feathers. Trans. W. S. Dallas. *Annals and Magazine of Natural History,* 3rd ser., 9:261–267.

Waldmann, M. 1970. A third specimen of a lower Cretaceous feather from Victoria, Australia. *Condor* 72:377.

Walker, A. D. 1972. New light on the origin of birds and crocodiles. *Nature* 237:257–263.

———1977. Evolution of the pelvis in birds and dinosaurs. In *Problems in vertebrate evolution,* ed. S. M. Andrews et al., vol. 4, pp. 319–358. London, Linnean Society.

Webb, M. 1957. The ontogeny of the cranial bones, cranial peripheral and cranial parasympathetic nerves, together with a study of the visceral muscles of *Struthio. Acta Anatomica* 38:81–203.

Wetmore, A. 1926. Fossil birds from the Green River deposits of eastern Utah. *Annals of the Carnegie Museum* 16(3–4):391–402.

———1934. Fossil birds from Mongolia and China. *American Museum Novitates* 711:1–16.

———1944. A new terrestrial vulture from the upper Eocene deposits of Wyoming. *Annals of the Carnegie Museum* 30:57–69.

———1960. A classification for the birds of the world. *Smithsonian Miscellaneous Collections* 39:1–37.

———1967. Re-creating Madagascar's giant extinct bird. *National Geographic Magazine* 132:488–493.

Whetstone, K. N., and L. D. Martin. 1979. New look at the origin of birds and crocodiles. *Nature* 279:234–236.

Willis, E. O. 1966. The role of migrant birds at swarms of army ants. *Living Bird* 5:187–231.

Williston, S. W. 1879. Are birds derived from dinosaurs? *Kansas City Review of Science* 3:457–460.

Index